The Spring of Butterflies

and other folktales
of China's minority peoples

The Spring of Butterflies

and other folktales
of China's minority peoples

translated by He Liyi

edited by Neil Philip

paintings by
Pan Aiqing and Li Zhao

Lothrop, Lee & Shepard Books
New York

First published 1985 in Great Britain
Text copyright © 1985 by William Collins Sons & Co Ltd.
Illustrations copyright © 1985 by William Collins Sons & Co Ltd.

Origination by Culver Graphic Ltd.
Printed and bound in Great Britain by Hazell Watson and Viney Ltd.
First U.S. Edition 1986
1 2 3 4 5 6 7 8 9 10

Library of Congress Cataloging in Publication Data
Main entry under title:
The Spring of butterflies and other folktales
of China's minority peoples.

1. Tales — China   2. Minorities — China
3. China — Social life and customs.
I. He, Liyi, 1930–
2. Philip, Neil.
GR335.S62 1986   398.2'0951   85-12887
ISBN 0-688-06192-3

Contents

Introduction   7

He Liyi: a biographical note,
    and a note on the artists   11

Acknowledgments   21

The Wonderful Brocade (Zhuang)   23

The Spring of Butterflies (Bai)   35

The Tibetan Envoy (Tibetan)   42

The Dougarda Brothers (Thai)   50

A Woman's Love (Uighur)   58

The Princess's Veil (Uighur)   75

The King and a Poor Man (Kazak)   82

The Story of Washing Horse
    Pond (Bai)   87

A Crane and Two Brothers (Tulong)   94

A Stone Sheep (Yi)   98

A Golden Fish (Uighur)   103

The Two Brothers (Naxi)   114

Green Dragon Pond (Bai)   119

"Never Heard of This Before" (Thai)   134

Notes on the stories   141

Introduction

The first thing to say about these stories is that they are not Chinese. They come from China, via Chinese, but they were all collected among minority peoples. The translator, He Liyi, is himself a Bai, from Yunnan in southwest China. Three of the tales, all telling the story behind a place-name, are Bai in origin. Most of the rest were collected from other minorities in Yunnan: the Yi, Naxi, Tulong, Thai and Zhuang. "The Tibetan Envoy" is a Tibetan story from neighbouring Szechwan; "The King and a Poor Man" is a Kazak tale from the far northwest, and "A Woman's Love", "The Princess's Veil" and "A Golden Fish" are all Uighur stories, again from the province of Xinjiang in northwest China.

All of these peoples lead very different lives, with different customs and different languages. What they have in common is that they do not belong to the Han Chinese who dominate Chinese culture. There are over twelve million Zhuang in the provinces of Yunnan and Guangxi (now the Guangxi Zhuang Autonomous Region); there are just over four thousand Tulong.

Three language groups are represented: Tibeto-Burman – Yi, Naxi, Tulong, Bai and Tibetan; Altaic (Turkic) – Uighur and Kazak; Thai – Zhuang and Thai. The different structures of these languages, as well as different social structures, mean that story-telling traditions vary, as does the flavour of the

7

stories told. Much of this variation has inevitably been ironed out in the many transitions these tales have been through since they last left a storyteller's mouth.

Many of the minorities have no script for their languages, or only a rudimentary one reserved for prayers and the like. These stories have been written down and published in Han Chinese, in a form approved (and probably "improved") by official Chinese folklorists, then translated by He Liyi, then lightly reworked by me. This last process, taking us even further from the words actually spoken, seemed to me to be justified only in so far as it served both the explicit purpose of He Liyi and the implicit purpose of the original oral storytellers: to give pleasure by telling a good story well.

My changes have been of three kinds: simple corrections of mistaken English; clarification of storyline when it was obscure; and minor alterations to inject vitality when I felt that the tales had been unduly battered somewhere in the chain of transmission. The aim has been to produce idiomatic and fluent stories which will appeal to English readers, while maintaining an alert respect for the originals and retaining as much as possible of He Liyi's idiosyncratic but flavoursome English.

As the biographical note shows, He Liyi's study of English was interrupted for nearly thirty years, during which time he was afraid to buy or even listen to a radio, had no books, and no opportunity to practise the language. Unsurprisingly, his English is sometimes stilted and sometimes incorrect.

Nevertheless his use of the language has powerful attractions. Some of his sentences make one smile out of mere quaintness: "Every now and then they were often found to be short of this or that." These instances I have, sometimes regretfully, removed. Just as often, his English has the freshness of our first taste of something new. No native English speaker would have translated the monk's injunction to his novices in "Green Dragon Pond" into He Liyi's tumbling monosyllables – "Just go, go, go, both of you go down to buy" – and no native English speaker could better them. His texts were remarkable most of all for their rhythmical felicity, and for their manipulation of sound. In "A Stone Sheep", for instance, I could not bring myself to delete his line, "Her feet were seriously pierced by stings." The meaning is clear, and the edge of strangeness reminds us that, despite familiarity, these tales come from cultures very unlike our own.

For the stories are, of course, familiar. Their components – impossible tests for hopeful suitors, terrible trials for faithful lovers, magical aid for honest toilers – their outcome – vice punished and virtue rewarded –and their method – the dream-like unfolding of the logic of images, not events – are those of folktales the world over.

At the junction of that familiar content and unfamiliar approach, a keen pleasure lies in wait.

Neil Philip
1984

Biographical Note

He Liyi was born in 1930, in a mountain village in Jianchuan county, a small district in the northwest of Yunnan province in southwest China. He is of Bai nationality, one of ten minority peoples in Yunnan. His grandfather, a stonemason, had eight children. The first seven were disregarded as "useless girls"; the eighth, He Liyi's father, was a son, so the family spared nothing to secure him an education. He became a policeman.

He Liyi writes, "Because of my father's police service, I had a golden opportunity to leave my home village in 1944 and complete my schooldays in Kunming (the capital of Yunnan). My father retired in 1948 and died in 1949, the year I entered Kunming Teachers' College.

"My mother was an ordinary village woman. She died in 1960, while I was 'reforming' my 'thoughts' on a state-owned farm near Kunming.

"I have one brother, who served as a junior officer in the Guomindang Army, but unfortunately joined an uprising before the communist troops came. As a result he was asked to join the People's Liberation Army, but he insisted on returning home. He became a farmer, but when the Land Reform movement started in our home county in 1950, he got a bad name: landlord. It was not until 1978 that his 'hat' (landlord) was formally taken off, and he was treated again as an ordinary commune member. He

11

is all right and enjoying a peaceful life now.

"As for my four young sisters, they are all ordinary commune members in my home county."

He Liyi learned his English ABC at school. He used to play at "teaching English". One day the teacher, Miss Xue, noticed this and, to encourage his interest, lent him an English-Chinese dictionary and an illustrated English children's story: Wilde's "The Happy Prince". She introduced him to her Professor at Kunming Teachers' College, and to his daughter, Miss Wu, who was already studying English at the college.

With their help He Liyi entered the college's English department. He spent each Sunday at Miss Wu's home; "Every now and then we would talk a few words about getting married." But in 1952, instead of becoming a teacher of English, she was sent to northeast China to study Russian for four years. Meanwhile He Liyi continued with his studies, encouraged by the dean of the English Department, Mr Chen, who like so many intellectuals "was cruelly treated and suffered a sad death during the Cultural Revolution."

Two months before he graduated in 1953, his cousin brought a village girl dressed in the Bai national costume to Kunming. It was Zhenjing, the daughter of his next-door neighbour at home. They had played together as children, and their parents had arranged their marriage. But such customs were dying, especially after the Revolution, and since He Liyi moved to Kunming in 1944 no mention had been made of the engagement. Now Zhenjing was left alone in the city, with only He Liyi to look after her. He tried to send her home, and she threatened to kill herself.

In He Liyi's first year at college, there were eighty students of English; when he graduated there were only seventeen. Of these, seven were sent to learn Russian, and ten, including He Liyi, were found office jobs in Yunnan. "No more chance to learn English. All my English books were locked in a box."

"As for the village girl, Zhenjing, sometimes I hated her, but at the same time, when I put myself in her position, I pitied her and loved her very much. She was not the person to blame; all our troubles were caused by feudal ideas."

They married, and in the time he could spare from his administrative job He Liyi set about teaching Zhenjing to speak, read and write Chinese. She learned rapidly. At first she worked cleaning the streets, then got a full-time job in a nursery school.

When Zhenjing's father heard of her job, he wrote that she should be looking after her own children. She was bringing shame on the family, doing "a slave girl's job. It would be much better to be a beggar in the street." He Liyi writes, "Such terms as 'Be a good wife' or 'a good mother', or 'Serve your husband faithfully' meant nothing but bear a large number of boys and girls quickly for the 'family honour', to glorify our ancestors."

Zhenjing stopped work, and she and He Liyi began to quarrel. Eventually he suggested that she return to the village. They obtained a formal divorce.

"Coming out of the court with the document in our hands, we walked shoulder to shoulder like a newly married couple."

The days before her departure were happy ones, and when they parted they exchanged presents: He Liyi gave her a fountain pen engraved with his name; Zhenjing gave him a pillow-case embroidered with their pictures, two swans, two hearts pierced on an arrow, and the words "We love in Kunming, 1955 Zhenjing".

In 1956 a committee of the Chinese Academy of Science was established in Kunming to study the minority peoples of Yunnan, and He Liyi worked for it, translating English material into Chinese. But in 1957 "Office work came to a stop. For several months we did nothing but hold meeting after meeting."

The Cantonese girl, Miss Wu, had meanwhile returned to Kunming to teach Russian. They decided to marry. On the day early in 1958 when the papers allowing the marriage came through, He Liyi was sent to a state-owned farm as a "bad element". "The car began to move as the girl arrived. We called to each other and waved our hands but we couldn't hear each other. It was the saddest goodbye."

The farm was not a prison. There were no warders or soldiers, there were three meals a day, and a small wage. The workers could not leave, but they could receive visitors. Miss Wu and her father came once, and sent parcels and encouraging letters, but after October 1961 he heard nothing.

In 1962 his "hat" was taken off: he was free to go.

He Liyi went to Kunming to look for Miss Wu, but she had gone to another province. He returned to his home village, after twenty years' absence. "The day I arrived home, so many villagers came to our house, and, Oh, too many questions to answer. As for my brother, he received me warmly at first. As days went by, when he learned I had returned poor, he became cold."

He Liyi went to see Shi, Zhenjing's father, who would not believe that they were divorced, and urged He Liyi to move in with him. He gave He Liyi a long letter from Zhenjing, recalling their year in Kunming, and telling him of her undying love. When she had returned from Kunming, she had put what she had learned to good use, and had become a doctor; she was now away having two years' extra training. "In Kunming I was a silly country girl; in our village I suddenly became the cleverest." She had had every success, but "in spite of that, I am very sad in my heart. The old man is my father but he never showed me a smiling face when I returned home. When I saw a mother playing with her children, my heart hurt, as if a knife was cutting it. When I saw a young couple working in the fields or walking together after supper, I could only take out my purse and look at the picture that was taken in Kunming."

He Liyi did not know how to answer. "I hated myself. I was ashamed of myself . . . I was too sad to eat or drink."

He wrote back to Zhenjing, telling her to keep up

her medical studies and to marry someone else: "The world today belongs to you."

Then one of his cousins found him a wife in another commune, a village girl who was unmarried at twenty-eight because she had been looking after her father. Her name was Cunniang.

They married and settled down in the new commune, and in 1963 they had a son. Next year a parcel arrived, posted from a military organization. It was full of toys, books and children's clothes. Inside the cover of one of the books he found Zhenjing's name, and the words "Keep secret".

Later a letter from Zhenjing explained everything. News of his marriage had made her ill: "It showed you do not believe in my true and persistent love." Now she herself was married to an army officer, a Han Chinese, and they had a baby girl. She sent as a present for He Liyi's son the inscribed pen he had given her in Kunming.

For the four years between 1966–69, He Liyi worked on a road-building project in Sichuan province. Then he returned to the village to work again in the fields, this time finding the work easy. He did not make contact with Zhenjing, in case he tainted her with his political disgrace.

In 1973, the provincial radio station began to broadcast English lessons. Before long, the local school started teaching English. He Liyi was appointed as teacher by the school authorities, but was blocked by officialdom because of his past. "I remember Zhenjing's words: Build hope on our coming generation. Facts taught me I had to pay attention to my children. I had to turn grief into strength. I began to teach my little boy English before he went to our village school."

Alongside his collective work on the land, He Liyi began to grow and sell his own vegetables, and to keep rabbits and bees. He also learned carpentry.

Selling his goods in the market, He Liyi came under attack as "a typical capitalist", but was saved from arrest by an army officer who bought a cock from him. When he got home, he found his wife Cunniang had also been attacked by market officials. She had been knocked down, and a tractor had run over her leg. She was taken to the hospital, but could not be taken through the gates unless 50 yuan was paid in advance. Just then an ambulance drew up, and a lady doctor got out of it and insisted on Cunniang being treated. It was Zhenjing, newly returned from Kunming. She had treated He Liyi's son ten years earlier, while he was in Sichuan, and recognized Cunniang from that time. She also asked her husband – the buyer of the cock – to send an army vehicle to take He Liyi and his son to the hospital. They were met there by Zhenjing's daughter, who told them that her mother had taken Cunniang to a bigger hospital. The 50 yuan was paid.

Cunniang was cured, and a new channel of communication opened between He Liyi and Zhenjing. The Cultural Revolution had failed; change was on the way. In the meantime, she wrote to him, "Be more careful. Speak less wherever you go. Lift your

17

hoe higher and dig the earth deeper. Keep your eyes and ears open and your mouth shut. Take care. Zhenjing."

He Liyi tried to lie low, but he was denounced as "a reactionary element . . . a false commune member . . . a smuggler . . . a capitalist . . . a running dog of American imperialism . . . a faithful grandson of Liu Shaogi."

"One day they organized a 'public show' of me through the villages near our commune. In those days, the so-called 'public shows' often took place. A group of young men in the village painted my face black and white like a circus clown. I was forced to put on a tall paper hat, and shoulder placards reading 'capitalist', 'bad element', 'running dog', 'rightist', and carry a gong and a gong-beater. I was ordered to walk ahead of everyone, from village to village, with lots of children following behind. It looked like a festival parade. If people gathered round, I had to make a confession."

In 1976 He Liyi once again tried to sell goods in the market: potatoes, fish and chairs which he had made. Once again he got into trouble, and once again Zhenjing and her army husband saved him.

"The English proverb, 'A friend in need is a friend indeed,' is perfectly true. In my own case, Zhenjing's friendship was a striking example. I have a thousand and one words to praise her special friendship. Really it was so touching that I simply didn't know where to find the most suitable words to express my heart of gratitude."

After the downfall of the Gang of Four, He Liyi and Zhenjing were able to express this friendship openly, and she encouraged him to resume his English studies.

He Liyi became a teacher in Jianchuan province. His pupils, like himself, are from minority ethnic groups whose first priority is learning to speak everyday Chinese. But, "I'll keep on troubling them with English." Cunniang sold a pig to buy him a radio, and he made contact with the BBC, whose Sara Lim encouraged him. She sent him an English-English dictionary, and "With Sara's modern weapon, I never stop attacking English."

He translated these local folktales and sent them to Derek Brooke-Wavell of the BBC's Chinese Section, who passed them on to Collins. He Liyi remains a teacher, "grateful to English friends, and longing for criticism from them." His address is He Liyi, Jian Chuan Second Middle School, Jian Chuan County, Tali, Yunnan Province, People's Republic of China.

The illustrations by Pan Aiqing and Li Zhao are the result of a competition organized by the BBC Chinese Service in 1982. After looking at many of the paintings submitted for the competition, Collins wrote to Pan Aiqing and Li Zhao and asked them if they would submit samples of their illustrations with a view to illustrating He Liyi's book. To Collins' delight when they replied, enclosing beautiful pictures, they said that they would like to illustrate the book together, as they were married.

They are both members of the Chinese Artists Association and graduated from Guangxi College of Fine Arts in 1982. There they were classmates and specialized in Chinese paintings. They live in Beihai City where Pan Aiqing is Arts Editor on the Beihai Newspaper and Li Zhao is an Arts Curator in the Beihai Cultural Palace.

The illustrations for this book have been painted jointly by them. They sent the roughs to He Liyi for approval and all correspondence with Collins has had to be translated into and out of Chinese by Zoë Chau of the BBC Chinese Service.

Acknowledgments

The publishers wish to thank the following people for their help in producing this book: Claire Chik, Laura Hitchins and Ralph Kiggell who personally delivered messages to He Liyi; Irene Andreae who advised on the spelling of Chinese names; Zoë Chau of the BBC Chinese Service who translated letters into and out of Chinese; and Derek Brooke-Wavell who was a constant source of help and advice over matters Chinese.

The Wonderful Brocade

Once upon a time on the plain at the foot of a huge mountain, there lived an old widow and her three sons.

The woman was very good at weaving brocades. The flowers, trees, birds and animals she wove on cloth were so lively that everyone wanted to buy her work.

One day, when the woman went to town to sell her brocades, she spied a wonderful picture in a shop. Coloured on that picture was a big house set in a pretty garden, with land stretching into the distance. There was an orchard, a vegetable plot, a fish pond, and lots of farm animals. She couldn't stop looking at it. The more she looked, the happier she felt. Usually she spent all her money on rice, but that day she bought less and took that wonderful picture home.

On her way home she sat down many times to look at the picture. She said to herself, "How happy

23

I should be if I could live in a wonderful place like this."

When she got home she showed the picture to her sons, and they too got all excited by it.

The mother asked her biggest son, "Do you think we could live in this good place?"

He said, "That is just a dream."

The mother turned to her second son. "Do you think we could live in this good place?"

He said, "Not yet. Perhaps when we die we shall be born again there for a second life."

The mother said to the youngest son, "I *shall* die if I cannot live in that good place."

The youngest son thought for a while and comforted his mother with these words: "You are such a good weaver, mother. You can almost make a picture come alive. Copy this scene onto a cloth. When you look at it, you will feel as though you are living in the good place."

She said, "You are right. I will do it or I shall die."

The mother bought some colourful silk thread, set up the loom and started to weave the wonderful picture.

Day followed day, month followed month, and still she wove.

The biggest son and the second son didn't like it. They often stopped their mother saying, "You have woven for months and sold nothing. Why should we do all the work, gathering firewood to sell for rice? We are tired and want to rest."

But the youngest son said to them, "Let mother

alone. She will die if she doesn't weave. If you think that getting firewood is too heavy or too much trouble for you, leave that job to me."

And from then on the two older brothers stayed at home, while the youngest boy went far and wide to get firewood, by day and night. Only he kept the four of them alive.

The mother also kept on weaving by day and night. In the evenings, instead of lighting a lamp, they burned some of the wood which the youngest son had fetched. The smoke was so thick that the mother's eyes hurt. In spite of that, the old woman kept on weaving ceaselessly. After a year her tears dropped on the cloth, and where they fell she wove a little river and a round pond. Two years later, blood dropped down from her eyes, and there she wove a red sun and many fresh flowers.

She worked and worked for three years before the brocade was finished.

What a beautiful brocade it was!

The large house had blue tiles, green walls and red pillars. Behind a yellow gate there was a big garden full of flowers in bloom. In the middle of the garden there was a pond with fish swimming to and fro. To the left of the house there was an orchard. The trees were full of red fruit, and on their branches were all kinds of birds. To the right of the house there was a vegetable plot, bursting with green vegetables and yellow melons. Behind the house were fields of rice and corn. A clean stream passed in front of the house, and the red sun shone above it.

"Oh, this cloth is really very beautiful," the three brothers praised.

The mother gave her waist a stretch and rubbed her aching eyes to look at the cloth. She began to smile.

But just then a strong wind gusted from the west and snatched the wonderful brocade up into the sky, and carried it away to the east.

The woman rushed after it, waving her arms. She was crying. She watched the wonderful brocade disappear, till there was only blue sky to be seen.

The old woman fainted outside the door.

The three brothers helped her into bed. She drank a bowl of herbal tea, and felt a bit better. She said to the biggest son, "Go to the east and find the cloth. It is as precious as my life."

The biggest son agreed to go. He put on a pair of straw sandals and set out for the east. After a month's walk he arrived at the foot of a huge mountain.

There he found a cave, and on the right side of the cave there was a stone horse with its mouth wide open as if it wanted to eat the red berries from a nearby tree. A white-haired old woman was sitting at the cave entrance. She asked, "Boy, where are you going?"

The biggest son replied, "I am looking for a wonderful brocade. My mother spent three years weaving it, and it was taken away to the east by a strong wind."

The white-haired old woman said, "That beautiful brocade was stolen by the spirit maidens of the Sun Mountain of the East. They saw your mother had woven a wonderful brocade and sent the wind to fetch

it to them, so they could copy it. It is very hard to find their palace. First, you must pull out two of your teeth and put them into the mouth of my stone horse. With the teeth, it can eat the berries, and when it has eaten ten berries you may ride on its back and it will take you to the Sun Mountain of the East.

"On the way, you must cross a fiery mountain. Oh, the fierce flames of that mountain cannot be described. Do not flinch as the stone horse carries you through the flames: you must bear all hardship, and be silent. You'll be burnt to a little flake of ash if you utter a sound.

"After you get through the flames, you'll come to a wide sea. Gales will buffet you, and rough ice will stab at you. All this you'll have to bear and say nothing. If you shiver or if you speak you'll be buried at the bottom of the sea.

"Beyond the sea is the Sun Mountain of the East. There you may ask the spirit maidens to return your mother's brocade."

The white-haired old woman looked at his face, and said with a smile, "My boy, you cannot stand these hardships. Don't go. I'm going to give you a box of gold with which to lead a better life."

She brought an iron box full of gold from the cave. The biggest boy took it and turned back.

As he walked home, he thought, With this little box of gold, I could lead a rich life. But if I take it home, there is not enough to make four people rich. It is much better for one person to have all of it than to let four people share it.

And so, instead of taking the box of gold home, he made up his mind to go to the big city.

The mother's illness grew worse. She waited in bed for two months, but the biggest son didn't come back. Calling the second son, she said, "Go to the east to search for the wonderful brocade. That cloth is my life-work."

The second son nodded. He put on his straw sandals and set out for the east. After a month's journey, he reached the mountain. There the old woman still sat near the cave mouth. She told him of the dangerous journey as before. The second son touched his teeth, imagining the scorching flames and the roaring waves, and his face quivered.

The old woman gave him another box of gold. He took it and went to the city, just as his brother did.

The mother lay in bed for another two months. She couldn't eat, and she was as skinny as a stick. She just sobbed bitterly as she lay looking to the east. She looked so hard and cried so much she went blind.

One day the youngest son said to her, "Mother, my two brothers have gone and nothing has been heard of them. Some unlucky thing must have happened to them on the way. Let me go. I'm sure to bring the beautiful brocade back."

The mother thought for a while and then said, "All right. You go but you must take good care of yourself on the way. The neighbours will look after me."

The youngest son put on his straw sandals and

marched bravely to the east. In less than a month, he arrived at the foot of the mountain and found the old woman, still sitting in front of the cave.

The old woman told him what she had told his brothers. She said, "My child, your two brothers have taken a box of gold each. You can have a box just like theirs."

But the youngest son struck his breast and said, "No, I'm going to get the beautiful cloth." Then he picked up a rock and hit himself in the mouth with it. He took out two of his teeth and put them into the mouth of the stone horse. The big stone horse stirred. It began to eat the berries, and when it had eaten ten, the youngest boy leapt up on its back, gripping fast to its mane. The stone horse neighed a long neigh and off they started for the east.

After three days they reached the blazing mountain. The flames shot upwards. They licked him fiercely, but the boy stood the pain and said nothing. It took them about half an hour to get through the fire. After the fire came the roaring sea, with its sharp and freezing waves coming one after another. They sank icy teeth in him, but the boy stood the pain and said nothing. And at last the stone horse stepped from the sea onto the slopes of the Sun Mountain. The boy stood in the warm sunlight and smiled and smiled.

A cheerful clatter was coming from the palace of the Sun Mountain. The boy walked into the hall, and saw a group of ravishing spirit maidens clustered around a cloth. His mother's brocade was displayed in front of them, and they were copying it.

They were very surprised to see him. He told them he had come for the brocade. One of them said, "Our work will be finished this evening. You can have the cloth back tomorrow morning. But for tonight, please, stay here."

The boy said, "Yes." The maiden gave him magic fruits to eat. Oh, they had such a tang!

The boy was so tired that he fell asleep on a chair. The spirit maidens worked on. When dark fell, they just hung a pearl from the ceiling, which made the hall as bright as daytime. They were all kept busy in their hurry to finish the cloth.

A maiden dressed in red was quicker than the rest, and she finished her job first. She went to compare her work with the mother's brocade, and she thought the mother's skill was much greater than hers. Just look: the sun was redder, the fish pond was clearer, the flowers fresher and the animals more life-like.

The maiden dressed in red said to herself, "How nice it would be if I could live in the good place shown on this brocade." As the other maidens were still busy, she took some more silk thread and embroidered a picture of her own on the old woman's cloth. It was a picture of herself, standing next to the pond and looking at the fresh flowers.

It was very late in the evening when the boy woke up. All the spirit maidens had gone to bed. Under the bright light of the pearl, he could see his mother's cloth on display. The maidens' copy was not finished. He thought, What if they do not give

31

me the cloth? My mother has been sick for so long. I cannot wait. I'd better take it and leave before they get up.

The boy stood up, folded the cloth and put it in his shirt. He walked out and jumped onto the horse's back. In the moonlight, they made their escape.

Once again, the boy and the stone horse crossed the raging sea and climbed over the fiery mountain. Soon enough, and not too soon, they found themselves back at the mouth of the cave.

The old woman was still there. She smiled, and said, "Get down, my child."

The boy dismounted. The old woman pulled out two teeth from the stone horse and fixed them back into the boy's mouth. The stone horse stiffened. It stood motionless by the tree, its mouth open by the berries.

The old woman gave the youngest son a pair of deerskin shoes. He put them on, and after a few paces he was home. His mother was lying, so skinny and shrivelled as a piece of dry firewood. She was moaning a little. Truly the old woman was going to die soon.

The youngest boy came to her bed and called, "Mother." He pulled out the wonderful brocade from his shirt. And as the cloth was unfolded before her, his mother found that she could see it. She got up then and there to look at the brocade on which she had worked for three whole years. She said, "My boy, it is too dark to appreciate it. Let's go out and look at it under the sunlight."

The mother and the boy walked out of the door and unfolded the cloth on the ground. There came a fragrant wind, and the wonderful cloth billowed and grew, getting wider and longer until it covered the ground for many miles.

The cottage they used to live in was gone. Instead of that poor shed, there was a grand building surrounded by a garden, an orchard and a vegetable plot, with crops and herds of cattle. Everything was just the same as in the wonderful picture. The mother and her youngest son were standing in front of the main gate.

Suddenly, the woman noticed a girl dressed in red looking at the flowers near the pond. She hurried to ask the girl who she was and what she was doing. The girl replied, "I am a spirit maiden. I embroidered my own picture onto the cloth. I would like to live here."

"You are welcome," said the mother.

And in time the youngest brother and the spirit maiden were married, and they all lived a happy life together. They invited all the poor people who lived nearby to come and share the good place, especially those who helped the mother when she was so ill.

One day two beggars came to the edge of the good place. These two beggars were the very same brothers who had gone to the city to spend their boxes of gold. They had enjoyed themselves eating and drinking whatever they wanted. Very soon their gold was gone, and they had to become beggars.

They saw the good place, and their mother smiling, and their young brother singing with his beautiful wife. They were ashamed to go in. Dragging their sticks in the dust, they walked away and away.

The Spring of Butterflies

There are nineteen peaks at Zansan in Dali. One of them is called Yunnong Peak (the peak where the clouds play). Beneath it there is a pond about ten metres across, surrounded by thickly covered trees and tall bushes, and, in spring, yellow flowers among the green leaves. This pond has a beautiful name: people call it "the Spring of Butterflies".

It wasn't always called "the Spring of Butterflies". Long ago, because the water was constant, and purer than other springs, and because nobody knew how deep it was, or had ever seen its bottom, the villagers who lived near it used to call it "the Bottomless Pond".

There lived by the side of this pond a farmer by the name of Lao Zhang. Lao Zhang had no relatives other than a daughter. He never went anywhere or did anything, year in, year out, except work, work, work on his little piece of land.

35

Wengu, his daughter, was eighteen or nineteen years of age. Her face was so beautiful that the prettiest flower couldn't be compared with her. Her eyes gleamed like stars in the sky. Her fine black hair cascaded like the leaves of a weeping willow. Her rosy cheeks were red as an apple. She was very kind, and her heart was as pure as the spring water. She worked hard alongside her father in the fields during the day, and in the evenings busied herself with weaving. There wasn't another girl in the country who could weave as well as Wengu. Her slender body was always occupied either in the field or at her loom.

Wengu was famed for her diligence and her beauty. Everyone talked of her; the girls envied and copied her, and the boys all dreamed of winning her love.

At that time there was a young woodcutter by the name of Xiana who lived at Yunnong Peak. He had no parents, and lived a poor and lonely life. Like the girl Wengu, he worked hard and long. His wisdom and quick intelligence outstripped that of Luban, the famous carpenter of ancient China. He was loyal and forthright. His singing voice was also incomparable: as graceful as a lark, as resonant as a nightingale. When he sang, the birds fell silent and the breeze hushed in the pines. The whole world stopped to listen to his song.

Xiana went to sell his firewood in town once a week, and he had to pass the Bottomless Pond each time he came down. Like most of the young men, Xiana was in love with Wengu. Every time, he would secretly watch out for her as he passed her home.

Wengu also loved Xiana. As soon as she heard him singing, she would stop everything to listen to his beautiful voice. She would look out of her window and watch him, off in the distance.

Days passed. Pure and real love was rooted deep between them.

One calm moonlit evening, Wengu met Xiana at the pond side. Under the moonlight they poured out their hearts to each other. From that evening, their shadows were seen often near the Bottomless Pond, and their footprints found beneath the trees around the water.

Now below the Zansan mountains, there lived a notorious local tyrant called Tyrant Wang. He was the chief ruler of Zansan and Dali Lake. He exploited and oppressed people cruelly. All his riches were stolen from the common people. Many soldiers worked for him, arresting people and destroying their property. The people's hatred of Tyrant Wang was as high as Zansan and as deep as Dali Lake.

Tyrant Wang heard tell of Wengu, and decided to steal the girl as his eighth wife.

With a gang of his hired ruffians, Tyrant Wang went looking for the girl at the Bottomless Pond. The old man Lao Zhang was seriously beaten, and they took Wengu away by force.

Like a greedy dog slavering over a titbit, Tyrant Wang said to Wengu, "There is uncountable silver and gold in my royal treasury. I have the best food in the world, and the most beautiful clothes. You alone will enjoy all these good things, if you agree to be my wife."

37

Wengu paid no attention to him, and said scornfully, "I promised to love Xiana, the woodcutter. My heart cannot be bought by your silver and gold. I don't care how much you have."

Tyrant Wang was furious, and said, "Well, my power is stronger than the heavens. I was born to rule others for ever. If I stamp my foot on the ground, the sky will fall or a mountain move. I have great powers. How can a woodcutter compare with that? You can never escape from my hands. Hear me."

Wengu became braver still. She said boldly, "I don't care how great you are. I'm not interested if you can bring down the sky or move a mountain. I love Xiana. Nobody can change my heart. It is as constant as the snowfall on the White Snow Peak. You want me to be your wife. That's impossible. It's just a daydream."

They argued for three days and nights. Tyrant Wang tried every way to make her agree, but Wengu still replied, "No." Finally Tyrant Wang gave his soldiers orders to hang the girl up by her arms till she saw sense.

That day Xiana walked down to the pond with a light heart. He thought he would meet Wengu by the pond, and talk with her. But he was not met by Wengu's smiling face. Instead he found only Lao Zhang, bruised and beaten. The old man died shortly after stammering out the details of what had happened.

Xiana was filled with pain and hatred. He hur-

riedly buried the old man and then sped to Tyrant Wang's palace, carrying an axe.

In the darkness, Xiana climbed over the high wall, and found Wengu tied up in a stable. He cut her ropes, and helped her over the wall.

Wengu and Xiana ran fast in the darkness. Tyrant Wang, with a rabble of soldiers, was close behind.

They ran up to the hills. Tyrant Wang followed them. They escaped into a valley, and the gang followed them down. Tyrant Wang called out in a proud and loud voice, "We'll capture you up in the air or underneath the earth. You'll never escape from my hands."

Wengu and Xiana ran to the edge of the Bottomless Pond. They were surrounded by the gang. Tyrant Wang ordered them to kneel down on the ground and surrender.

Now Wengu and Xiana embraced each other tightly. They replied with cold eyes, said nothing, but jumped down into the Bottomless Pond . . .

When the people living around the Bottomless Pond heard the fate of the young couple, they were first of all moved to tears. Then they were moved to anger. Carrying makeshift weapons on their shoulders, they marched into Tyrant Wang's palace and destroyed everything. They killed Tyrant Wang and all his men.

The next day, a large crowd gathered at the Bottomless Pond. They were going to search for the bodies of Wengu and Xiana. All of a sudden, the water in the Pond opened up. From its centre, a pair of fresh and charming butterflies flew out, one after the other. They flew above the pond as though they were trying to catch each other. Hundreds and thousands more butterflies followed them, and circled about the pair, flying everywhere above the pond and under the trees.

From that day on, people gave the Bottomless Pond a new name: Spring of Butterflies. Each year in spring, all sorts and sizes of multi-coloured butterflies come to dance above the water. The pond becomes a sea of butterflies. It is a mystery and a wonder.

The Tibetan Envoy

Many years ago, the emperor of the Tang dynasty had a most beloved daughter, the Princess Wencheng. When she was old enough to get married, all the neighbouring princes sent an envoy to the capital to propose. And the prince of faraway Tibet also sent an envoy: the wisest man in Tibet, and the most cunning.

There were seven envoys in all. All of them had the same aim, to win Princess Wencheng's love, but all were in doubt. Who would succeed? Nobody knew.

The emperor thought Tibet was too far away. It would be hard to visit his daughter there. He had no mind to let his daughter marry a Tibetan prince, though he could not refuse the Tibetan envoy openly. He held a meeting of his ministers, to consider how to reject the Tibetan prince's suit. They decided to set a hard marriage test. When the Tibetan envoy failed, perhaps he would go away and leave them to choose the princess a husband from among the neighbouring princes.

On the following day, five hundred mares and their foals were brought to the city square. The foals were driven into the centre of the square, and their mothers were tied up round the edge. Then the king declared, "All seven of the princes are as dear and useful to me as my hands and arms. I really wish I had seven princesses for them. Too bad. I have only one daughter. I don't know whom I should choose. So to be fair, I've brought five hundred mares and their foals here. Now you seven envoys, get busy matching up mothers and young. Then I'll consider the marriage."

The seven envoys began. The six local ones rushed about, each trying to lead the foals to the mares, but the Tibetan envoy just waited politely for them to finish. Every time the envoys led a foal to the mares, all the horses bucked and kicked and made a tremendous commotion. The foals were afraid to go near. None of the envoys could match up mare and foal.

At last the Tibetan envoy's turn came. The Tibetans are very experienced with horses; they know just about everything about them. So he didn't blunder around like the others. Instead he asked for food of the best quality to be brought to the mares. All the mares stopped kicking and ate peacefully till they couldn't eat any more. As soon as they were finished, they looked up and neighed loudly. That was a call for the foals to suckle. And the foals all ran to their own mother, all sucking, prancing, licking, or happily whisking their tails.

The emperor appreciated this envoy's quick wits

very much, but he still didn't want him to win. So he announced another test. "This envoy is really very clever, and I like him too, but that's not the end. I want to give you all another chance." He took out a piece of elegant green jade and said to the seven envoys. "This jade is as intricate as it is beautiful. Look carefully at it, and you will find a hole twisting and turning right through it. When one of you hangs this jade on a thread, I will consider the marriage."

The Tibetan envoy let the other six try first, but they all failed hopelessly. They tried all day but none of them could get the thread through. At last the Tibetan envoy was asked to try.

The Tibetan envoy caught an ant and tied the thread to its leg. Then he smeared a little honey on the exit hole of the jade. The ant smelled the honey, and very quickly got through the hole with the thread trailing behind. The Tibetan envoy tied the two ends together and passed the jade necklace to the king.

The emperor was very surprised. He had to think of a new test the Tibetan might fail. He said, "We will try another competition, so that each one of you will believe I take you seriously." Then he instructed a carpenter to take a log, and plane and polish the wood till each end looked identical. The log was shown to the envoys, and the king said, "Here is a log. Come and examine it. I want you to make out which end comes from the top of the tree, and which from the bottom. I don't want guesswork. If any of you can explain it correctly, the question of my daughter's marriage will be easily decided."

The six local envoys examined it first. One by one they stared at it, turned it, touched it, measured it, but none could make out which end was which. Finally they asked the Tibetan envoy's opinion.

The Tibetan envoy came from the mountains, so he knew that a tree is heavier nearer the root. He asked them to put the log into the river. It floated with the lighter end ahead, the heavier behind. He easily pointed out which was which.

The emperor was impressed by this clever solution, but he still did not want to send his daughter so far away. Therefore he called another meeting of his ministers. One of them suggested, "Your Majesty should choose three hundred beautiful girls and dress them in the same clothes as the princess. Stand them in a line. If this envoy can tell her apart from the others, it must be fate. I don't think he can do that. In this way your daughter will remain near you."

The emperor agreed to this, and declared, "To be fair to all the envoys, we must have one last test. I have three hundred girls, all dressed alike. The princess is among them. He who identifies her correctly wins her for his master."

Again the six local envoys tried first. They thought the most beautiful girl ought to be the princess, but she wasn't. All pointed out the wrong girl.

Meanwhile the Tibetan envoy was busy around the palace trying to learn about the princess. He had never seen her or heard anything specific about her. He had many friends in the palace. He visited the cart drivers, the serving men, the washerwomen, hoping to find out about the emperor's daughter. At last he met an aged laundress who knew about the girl, but told him, "I am afraid to tell you anything. Our king has a private magician who knows all secrets. He would find me out and I should die."

The Tibetan calmed her fears. "Madam, you may rely on me. Tell me all you know about her. Do as I say and no magician can find you out." Then he brought three white stones and placed them on the ground. Above these stones he fixed a large iron cauldron filled with water. Then he laid a bench across the cauldron, and sat the old woman on the bench. He gave her a brass trumpet and said, "Speak boldly through this. The wisest magician can only say, 'the speaker lives on a wooden mountain. This wooden mountain is on an iron sea. The sea is at the top of three white mountains. The speaker has a brass mouth.' The emperor can never find you. He will think that 'brass-mouth' must be a witch or a spirit. So, be brave and please tell me all the details you know."

The old woman chuckled at that. She told him without the least fear, "My gentleman, in the first place you must not point at the most beautiful girl. The princess isn't ugly but she is not the most beautiful one. She is a princess, so people usually say she is the nicest girl in the world. Second, don't point at the front row or the back row. That's too obvious. The king puts his daughter in the middle. Third, the princess has worn oil on her hair since she was a child. Bees like it, and often fly above her head. She likes the

bees, and never waves them away. The other girls have no oil, for the princess gets it from abroad. So if you see bees around her head, you may point at her and she will be just the right princess. That's the gossip among the courtiers. The cooks heard it from them. I washed the cooks' clothes, so I heard it from them. Now, my gentleman, that is all I can tell you. Good luck!"

The Tibetan envoy thanked her and went to make his choice. He was very careful. He didn't point at the back row or the front row, nor at the most beautiful girl. He studied the girls one at a time. At noon, he saw a golden bee dancing above a girl's head. The girl didn't mind the bee. She wasn't afraid of it, but watched it lovingly. The Tibetan envoy pointed straight at her and said, "This is the princess." And it was exactly just the real princess. The emperor and the other six envoys were amazed at his success.

The emperor thought: this Tibetan envoy had never seen the princess, so how did he know so much more about her than the other envoys? Somebody must have talked to him.

The emperor ordered his magician to find out the culprit. But the magician just talked a lot of nonsense.

The emperor could not help it. He had to say "yes", and allow the Tibetan envoy to talk to the princess face to face.

The Tibetan said to her, "Princess, I am very glad to know your father the emperor has promised to let our Tibetan prince marry the best princess on earth. As you are going away with me, the emperor will want to give you a lot of presents. Our Tibetan prince has everything you need. So don't take jewels and silks, but remember what I'm telling you now. Ask him for seeds of all the chief grains. With them we shall make our land fruitful, which is a gift more precious than gold and silver."

The princess took his advice. Amazed at his daughter's request, the emperor gave her five hundred horses loaded with grain seeds to take with her to Tibet.

The Dougarda Brothers

In a Thai village there lived an old widow. She lived on
a little piece of land with her two shabby sons. These
two brothers had no names. The villagers called them
the Dougarda brothers, which just means "the paup-
ers". They didn't mind the nickname. Indeed they
called themselves Big Dougarda and Little Dougarda.

The Dougarda brothers often felt so sad, when they
saw their mother go hungry, that they would hide
away and weep. Their mother only ate the corn they
left. So to make her eat more, they left half of each
meal. But when she saw so much corn left after each
meal, the mother just cooked less food. So they asked
her to eat first, and eat as much as she liked before they
began. But she would never eat more than a little. They
tried many times but couldn't find a way to make their
mother eat till she was full. At last, they decided to go
and seek their fortune, and not come home till they had
earned a bag of gold. Then they could make their
mother live a happier life.

The Dougarda brothers left home and went to a prosperous place where they stayed for nearly two years. They toured round all the villages and markets in the area, looking for work. They wore rags and ate rough food. Gradually they saved a lot of money. Every time they saved a piece of gold, they put it in their bag. The days passed, and the bag became heavier each passing day.

Such a bagful of gold made the Dougarda brothers sleepless. They were forever making plans: how they would take the gold home; how they would build a new house near the river; how they would make their mother happy, and have vegetables for every meal. The more they planned, the more restless they became.

So they set off for home. To prevent bad people guessing they were carrying gold, they covered the gold with a slithery pile of eels, and then wrapped the gold and eels in the leather bag. The brothers carried the bag on a bamboo pole. On the way home, they had to cross a mountain. Instead of travelling along the road, they took a side route through the forest.

The sun was blazing hot. The birds were too hot to fly in the sky, but were stuck on the branches with their mouths open. The two brothers toiled on up the mountain slope. Their skin was burnt and split. Bubbles were coming out of Little Dougarda's mouth. He really couldn't go any further. But there was nowhere to stop. So Big Dougarda wetted Little Dougarda's mouth with water, and hoisted him on to his back. Piggy-back, they climbed the mountain.

51

On the other side of the mountain there was a little bamboo house, on a little rocky plot of land, in which an old man called Bosankang lived with his wife. They were too poor even to buy a new water jar if their old one broke.

The sun was setting when Big Dougarda staggered out of the woods with Little Dougarda on his back. He went up to the bamboo house and asked the old man to put them up for the night. The old woman smiled, "Oh, welcome to our home, dear birds! You can sleep here, and welcome." But Bosankang shut her up, and said, "You silly woman. They'd just burn a lot of our firewood."

Big Dougarda begged and begged, and finally Bosankang did let them sleep by the fireside.

That evening Little Dougarda burnt with fever. He groaned the whole night through. Big Dougarda could do nothing but feed him cold water and pray. When the sun rose, Little Dougarda was too sick to move. Big Dougarda sobbed painfully. He was afraid his young brother would die before seeing their mother. He decided to carry his brother home and leave the gold. He took out a little piece of gold for the journey, and put it in his pocket, and then he sewed the bag up again. He said to Bosankang, "My kind host, you have treated us like our parents. My young brother is seriously ill. I must carry him home. In this bag are some eels which we intend to offer to the Rain God. We ask you not to touch it. Just let it hang where it is. I'll come back and fetch it in five days."

Now Bosankang had seen a glint of gold earlier. He said, "Oh yes, you can leave your eels here." Simple, trusting Big Dougarda bowed many times, and left the bamboo house, carrying his brother on his back.

Four days later, Little Dougarda was well again, and both the brothers returned to the bamboo house. Entering the house, the two brothers gave a parcel of gifts to the old couple, and kept on thanking them for their kindness. Finally, they asked for their bag. Bosankang gave it to them with a curious smile. The Dougarda brothers dusted the bag. Then they picked it up. It seemed very light. Big Dougarda put his hand into the bag, and shrieked. There was nothing except a couple of dry eels in it. No more gold!

Big Dougarda said, "Our kind host, what has become of our gold?"

"Gold?" asked Bosankang loudly. "Gold? On your departure, didn't you say clearly that your bag was full of eels to offer to the Rain God?"

Big Dougarda and Bosankang scolded and argued for hours, but to no result. Eventually, the Dougarda brothers frogmarched the old couple to see the king.

The wise king saw that this was a tricky case. So he ordered his guards to take the four to a room in the palace where a feast would be served in their honour. He asked both sides to eat and drink as well as they could. As for his judgment, he would give it next morning, when the sun's rays touched the largest pillar in the palace.

The two Dougarda brothers were disappointed to hear the king's words. Many plates of mouth-watering food were served, but they had no heart to taste them. They simply sat at the table and cried. As for the old couple, they bowed and scraped, and endlessly praised the wisdom of the king. Between praises, they cleaned up every scrap and drank up every drop which had been brought to the table. Then they slipped under the table and fell asleep.

Just before dawn a bugle call rent the air. The four were brought to court. The king said to them, "I've decided you're all guilty. I'm going to punish all four of you by making you carry my biggest drum around the woods." That was the king's word. They had to obey.

The king's guards brought out two large ancient heavy drums. The Dougarda brothers shouldered one; the old couple the other. Then they carried the drums along the routes pointed out by the king.

The drums were the biggest ones in the palace. They were so heavy that the old couple could hardly breathe. As they climbed a slope, the wife grumbled and scolded the old man. "Listen to me, Bosankang, whatever made you steal that gold? Did a poisonous white ant or a snake bite your heart?"

The old man replied, "You silly woman! Do you know how long we can live on that bag of gold? Generations!"

Bosankang's wife was exhausted and didn't care what her husband was saying. She was in a real temper. She shouted, "You kept me away when you buried the gold, but now I have to help you carry this heavy drum. It isn't fair. I won't carry it any further."

Then the old man said in a hurry, "Let's not argue. Not after twenty years of happy marriage. How can I carry this drum all by myself? I'll let you into the secret. I buried their gold under the tea tree with three branches. Help me carry the drum, and I'll let you have half the gold."

His wife was happy to carry on then, and they kept going through the thick woods. They had only stopped for a short break when they overheard two men sighing.

"Oh, my dear young brother. We've only ourselves to blame. But we've not been blessed with much luck. I suppose that's life: something very good to eat has come near our lips, but somehow or other we've dropped it."

"My brother, forgive me please. It's all because of my sickness. We would never have asked such a wicked old man to look after our gold if I hadn't fallen ill that day."

"The common people have talked a great deal about our king's wisdom and his outstanding ability. People say he is like an eagle. That means he can see and judge everything on earth. But in our own case, I doubt it. He seems more like a farmyard hen than a soaring eagle. He couldn't find out who stole the gold. Instead he's punished us, and made us carry this old drum. Ah well, life is funny."

Bosankang put his hand over his wife's mouth as the brothers went past. "Let's hide and let them go first," he whispered.

The rays of the rising sun were shining on the tallest

pillar in the palace when the drum carriers returned. The king ordered them to appear again before him. He said to the four, "I'll give you one last chance to tell the truth. I'll cut off five fingers if you lie." Then he turned to the Dougarda brothers. "Did you really lose a bag of gold?"

"Oh king, we left it in their home."

The king turned to the old couple. "Did you steal their bag of gold?"

"Oh king, we saw no gold, only eels. Cut off all our fingers if anyone can prove we are thieves."

The king said, "Now, all of you pay attention. There is more evidence to hear." Then two of his guards were ordered to open the old, large drums, and out of each drum came a man, holding a pen and a piece of paper on which all the conversations on the way had been taken down.

Bosankang and his wife fainted clean away when they saw there was a man in the drum. The papers were handed to the king.

The king sent someone to dig up the bag of gold which had been buried by Bosankang, and return it to the Dougarda brothers. At the same time, he ordered his guards to cut off five of Bosankang's fingers.

"Just like our king," said the common people. "As wise and harsh as an eagle."

A Woman's Love

If a woman has won true love, it lasts her life and never fails. Nothing on earth can spoil it. But, if it be untrue, nothing can help her. Now I'm going to tell you about the love of a woman. This woman lived a poor life in the countryside, but she was clever and beautiful. Her skill at embroidering flowers was second to none.

She fell in love with a man when she was a little girl. Like her own family, that man had only a single room for a home. He had scarcely anything he could call his own. But he laboured hard with his hands, and never went hungry. He wasn't smart or wise. He was just an ordinary man. Everyone in the district knew he was straight as a die. He never told a lie, and he believed whatever he was told. The girl understood all this, but she loved him just the same. Her parents liked him too, and so the couple were engaged to be married.

It was common knowledge in the countryside that a

good girl couldn't stay unnoticed. Talk of her would spread till it came at last to the king's ears. With this girl it was the same. The king hadn't seen her. Though he was the leader of the country, he never went into the countryside. But he heard about her, and that was enough.

This is how it happened. Some of the toadies who tried to please the king by doing little services for him, showed him the girl's embroidery. He knew at once she must be a special girl. So he thought, she may be beautiful: then she would amuse me for quite a while. And if she is ugly or silly, I can just throw her aside and look for another one to play with.

Soon the king's minister arrived at the girl's home. "Good luck has come to the girl," he announced. "Our king wants to marry her."

The father said, "My daughter is already engaged. The marriage was her own choice. Don't bother me. Go and ask her."

The minister went to see the girl. Well, being a king's messenger, he had a tongue like a nightingale. He said a great number of good things, but the girl wasn't taken in. She said in a firm voice, "Go back. Please convey my thanks to the king. I don't want to marry him. You know I am a girl from a poor home. I want to marry a working man. I don't want to live in a palace and do nothing. A king, to marry a village girl from a poor family! Oh, it's no good at all. It would ruin his reputation." The minister was at a loss to find suitable words to answer her speech. With a heavy heart he reported it to the king.

The king was full of anger. "I'll get her sooner or later."

The girl married the poor man. They worked hard and made plans for their home. Gradually they saved eight silver coins. The girl said, "We mustn't waste this money. Take it to town and buy some cotton thread."

The man bought some cotton thread, and day and night the girl worked to embroider four ribbons. Her nimble hands made exquisite pictures. They sold the four ribbons for sixteen silver coins. The man used twelve coins to buy food, and four to buy more thread. The girl worked harder still, making beautiful ribbons. Soon they had earned forty coins. The girl said, "Buy me some coloured thread and I'll embroider a colourful bedspread."

When the bedspread was ready, she sent the man to sell it in town. "You must sell it for twenty silver coins. There are forty streets in our town and you may sell it in any street you like. Bring it back home if nobody wants to buy it. Remember this: you must not go to the forty-first street."

This bedspread was a rare and precious thing. People made a circle round it in the street, and jostled to see it. But though many admired it, none could pay twenty silver coins. It was hard to find a man rich enough to afford twenty coins for a bedspread. The husband walked up and down and nobody wanted to buy it. Late in the afternoon he thought of going home, but he was troubled as he thought how his wife had spent so much time on it and now nobody wanted to buy it. She will be very sad, he thought to himself. In order not to let her down, I should think of a way to sell it, and return home a little later than usual. He forgot what his wife had told him and stepped into the forty-first street.

The forty-first street was full of handsome buildings, but there wasn't a soul about. Now he realized why he was forbidden to come here. It must be where the palace officials lived. Just as he was about to turn back, a crowd of people spilled into the street through the gates. They were all dragging dogs or carrying eagles on their wrists. They looked powerful and proud. The king was riding a horse. As soon as he saw the man, he said, "What are you doing here? Don't you know this is the forty-first street?" His voice boomed like an ancient bell.

The man said, "Sorry, I didn't know. Here, I'll be off right away." But as he turned to go, the king caught sight of the bedspread.

"What's that in your hand?"

He answered, "Nothing. It's only a bedspread."

"Let me see," said the king.

The man unfolded the bedspread, and a pack of trouble with it. The king had seen the girl's handiwork once before, and this beautiful bedspread was obviously embroidered by her. It couldn't be denied. The king looked at the man standing beside him and hated him very much. "Who embroidered this?"

The man didn't know what to say. Instead of replying with a smart lie, he just opened and shut his mouth. Then he said, "I embroidered it." All the people around laughed, and he grew even more worried and awkward.

The king said, "Tell me the truth. You needn't be afraid. Who made it?"

He said, "It was made by my sister."

"I know this man," said one of the courtiers. "He has no sister."

The king's face turned serious. "I want no more of your nonsense. Speak out the truth. Quick, man!"

It was impossible to lie. He had to tell the truth. "My wife made it."

The king nodded, smiling. "A wonderful bedspread it is. How much do you want?"

He answered, "Twenty silver coins."

The king took the bedspread and paid him twenty coins, saying, "Tomorrow I'm going to hunt in the woods and I plan to take a rest when I pass your village. You must prepare something for me to eat."

On his way home, the more he thought the more the man regretted neglecting his wife's words. He asked himself many times why he had to go to the forty-first street; why he had to sell it there . . .

He handed all the money to his wife but he looked so unhappy she knew something unusual must have happened. She asked, "My dear, what makes you so sad?"

The man couldn't hide the truth, and he told her the whole story. After hearing it all, she was upset, and complained, "I told you not to go there, and you turned a deaf ear. Now, as you see, more trouble will come." The man was so distressed. He blamed himself. His eyes were filled with tears of shame. On

seeing this, the girl forgave him, and she comforted him, "Never mind. I'll hide myself when they come tomorrow. Say, 'She has gone out,' if they want to see me."

The next day the king truly came to their village and entered their house, calling loudly for tea to be served. He thought the lady of the house would have to come and make him the tea, but it was the man who came. The king said, "Tell your wife to make tea. I have more to ask you."

He replied, "My wife has gone away."

The king's face turned angry. Then he realized it was a simple trick. Certainly, she was hiding. So she thought she could run away from his hands? He turned kind. "Never mind, come here. Let's drink some wine together." The man thought the king was sincere. And as it was a rude thing to refuse a king's offer, he drank the wine, which was specially strong. Soon he was as drunk as a lord, and would not wake up for three or four days.

An order was given to search the room. Their home was only a single, narrow room. There weren't many hiding places. She was soon found.

The king was amazed at her beauty. No wonder people talked about her everywhere. Whoever saw her would fall in love with her. Naturally the king wanted her. He talked very big, and offered to do so many good things for her, but the girl refused him completely. "I am married. My husband is still living and I love him. I'll never change my mind to love another man, even if you kill me."

The king was very angry. He could do nothing except order his followers to tie her on horse-back by force. He thought he could have everything he wanted. As for the girl, she only thought of her drunk husband. How would he find her when he woke up, if they took her away? An idea appeared in her mind. She said to the king, "You have to grant me a favour if you are determined to marry me."

The king was very pleased. "Oh, tell me quickly. It needn't be just one favour. You are welcome to ask as many favours as you like."

The girl said, "It is the custom in our village that any woman who leaves her husband for another has to put cakes and water by the wayside for the spirits. If we neglect it, bad luck will come."

The king said, "Certainly, certainly. Do everything as you wish."

Then the girl made some special cakes, and left a few in front of her husband, with a secret mark pointing the direction she was forced to go. Next to the cakes she placed a bowl of water. The king took her away. But at intervals until they reached the king's palace she left cakes and water by the road.

Three days later, the man woke up and found himself alone. He knew the king had made a fool of him. His wife was kidnapped. But when he saw the secret mark on the cakes, he knew what to do. He ate the cakes and drank the water, and then set out to look for her. He walked the whole way, stopping to eat the cakes and drink the water on the route, and following the secret marks. They led him straight to the king's palace.

The walls of the palace were very high, and guards watched the gate all the time. It was hard to get in. For days and nights he did nothing but wander about the high walls. Then he met an old woman who asked him what he was looking for. The old woman looked kind and friendly, so he told her the truth. She said, "I'll give you a coin with which to buy some things girls need – thread, needles, looking-glasses, combs. Stand by the gate and cry your wares. You might chance to meet her."

The king wanted to marry her as soon as they got to the palace. But the girl said, "Waiting sharpens desire. Give me some time. You mustn't come to my room. There is no hurry." She gave the king a look which took away his speech.

A few days later, while the king was out hunting, the girl heard a hawker crying his wares by the gate. It was her husband's voice. She went to the gate. She was so happy to see him, but he couldn't recognize her, for her face was covered by a veil. She told him to come closer, so she could see what he had for sale. She looked at his trinkets, and let him know who she was. Then, at a moment when there was nobody nearby, she whispered, "Take these two coins and use them to buy two horses. Wait for me in the evening outside this wall in three days' time." She handed him the money, and whisked back through the gate. It was done secretly. No one saw them.

Returning from the hunt, the king paid her a visit, but she was not pleased. "Who has offended you?" asked the king.

The girl made an ugly pout. "It is you! You carried me off, but why am I here? I haven't the least authority here."

The king took out forty-one keys there and then, and said, "Here you are. Now you have charge of everything." She took the keys and began to smile a little smile. The king said, "Well, how much longer must I wait?"

The girl replied. "Just three more days. Be patient."

Next day when the king was again out hunting, she took her chance, unlocked the stable door and, choosing two good horses, ordered a servant to sell them at the market. Her husband bought them with his two silver coins.

The third day came. That evening, the husband brought the horses and waited for her outside the palace wall. The more he waited the more he worried. Where was she? He got so tired with waiting and worrying that he fell asleep beneath the wall.

Just then, the infamous bald-headed man of the town staggered by, and paused at the unusual sight of a sleeping man with two horses at midnight. The drunken bald-headed man was about to wake the sleeper and question him when two parcels dropped down from above, followed by a lithe figure. It was the king's new lady! The bald-headed man thought, Something is up.

She was in such a whirl she didn't look closely at the man standing by the horses, just told him to hurry up and tie the parcels to the saddle. She jumped up and rode off, and the bald-headed man rode just behind her. The moon shone brightly to light their way as they fled far from the king's palace.

After a long time they took a rest. The girl let her horse idle as she tidied her hair. She asked, "Did everything go all right?" The bald-headed man mumbled in reply. He was afraid to answer in a loud voice. The girl knew something had gone wrong. She peered at her companion. Oh! Instead of her husband, she was frightened to see the infamous bald-headed man of the town. She blamed herself for setting off so recklessly. She had only escaped into the hands of another bad man.

The girl wasn't downhearted. As they rode, she thought of many ways to cope with the situation. When dawn came, she said to him, "I've been thinking. To be blunt, I'd made up my mind to go off with the first man I saw, but I must tell you the truth. I don't like your bald head. It's ugly and a disgrace. Take these five coins and fetch me a big pan of oil. Hot oil is a sure cure for baldness. As soon as your hair grows again, we'll get married. How is that?"

The bald-headed man was overjoyed. He was in luck! He was going to marry a beautiful woman and get his hair back too. Immediately he bought a big pan full of oil at the nearest village. He gathered some firewood and heated the oil. When he sat with his bald head uncovered for the cure, the girl picked up the pan and poured the boiling oil on it, and killed him. She served him no worse than he had served others.

The girl rode on alone for some distance, till she met four hunters. As soon as they saw her, they began to argue. This one said, "I will marry her." That one said, "No, I will." And the others said, "Let me." "Let me."

The girl stopped them all. "What's the use of arguing with one another? No matter how you shout, I can't marry all of you. Let me see. Give me a bow and some arrows. I'll fire in four directions, and he who brings back an arrow first will marry me."

The hunters were very glad to settle their dispute with this race. Each of them was confident of success. They said, "That is very good. All right. Fire away."

The girl took the bow and shot four arrows as far as she could. But when those four hunters brought the arrows back, she was a long way off. All they won was sore feet.

She rode on and on again, till she met four gamblers. They too quarrelled, and all insisted on marrying her. The girl said, "Now listen to me. I'll give you a bowlful of wine each. He who drinks it all in one gulp but doesn't get drunk will marry me." The gamblers were well used to drink, and all agreed. But she gave them the king's strong wine, and they all fell fast asleep. All they won was sore heads.

Now the girl knew that it was a hard thing for a girl to travel alone. So she opened one of the parcels she had brought from the palace, and took out some men's clothes to disguise herself as a gentleman. Then she rode on safely till she came to a city.

It was a queer place. All the people were dressed in colourful clothes and looking up at the sky. They were all carrying big pieces of meat. They were

69

pushing and shoving and running up and down. She asked one of them, "What has happened, and what are you all doing?"

He explained, "Our king has died. His 'Bird of Happiness' has been released today. We are looking for the bird in the sky. The man on whom the bird chooses to land will become our new king. The meat is to tempt it."

As the man was speaking, the Bird of Happiness swooped low. People began to cheer, all hoping that the bird would bring them happiness, but after circling the crowd, the bird alighted on the shoulder of the girl dressed up as a man. All the people threw away their meat and shouted hurrah! Of course they all begged her to enter the palace.

Well, she had never thought that such a thing could happen to her. Truly she had never dreamed it. She didn't wish to do it, but their invitation couldn't be refused. They said that this custom had been handed down from generation to generation. Anyone who objected to it would be thrown into prison.

She became their king. Theirs was a big and powerful nation. Even that bad king who had kidnapped her was under its rule.

The girl received people's congratulations and set out learning how to rule. She dealt with everything fairly, and relied on common sense not clever arguments. All admired her. People said, "How happy we are now with such a good king." It was she who had brought happiness to the common people. So the people hoped she too would find happiness of her own. They said, "Our king, you are still single. It would be well for you to find a girl and get married."

She replied, "There is no hurry about that. It's early yet for me to get married. I'll let you know when I find the right girl." So the question of the king's marriage was left aside.

One day as she was studying something in her office, a high minister came to her, and said, "Four hunters have come to appeal to you, saying that a lady promised to marry them, but then ran away. Now they want to know whether she came here. What do you think?"

The king said, "The first thing is to put them in prison, and then wait until we find the lady." The minister did as she said.

A few days passed, and the minister came to report another case. "Another four men came to appeal to you, also saying a certain lady agreed to marry them but cheated them in the end by making them drunk."

The king said, "Let's wait. Put them in prison. We can't do anything till we find the lady."

A few days later, the bad king who was under the new king's rule arrived. Usually with the lesser kings, she would receive them pleasantly. But she knew who this little king was. Oh, she was full of hatred and anger. The bad king said, "There's a little matter on which I'd like your help."

The king said, "I'm too busy. Tell my minister what you want." She showed him the door.

A little while later the minister found her and said, "He told me that a lady promised to marry him, but she escaped. He was told that she came to this country."

The king said angrily, "Oh, nothing but looking for a lady all the time. I'm tired of it. Put him in prison. He can cool his heels there till we find the lady."

The minister was surprised to hear this decision. He thought that to throw a neighbouring king into prison wasn't a nice thing; but the king sounded so determined that he couldn't question it. And so the minister did just as she had ordered.

A few days passed. The minister reported, "Today again another man has come looking for a lady. He is young and poor. Shall I put him in prison too?"

The king said, "Wait. Bring him to me here."

The minister could not understand all this, but he did as she said. The king glanced at the man, and saw he was just the man she had been longing for every day and every night. That young poor man was the man whose absence had robbed the king's food of savour and her sleep of restfulness. It was her husband. But though the king knew him, the young man couldn't recognize his wife.

All the courtiers were asked to leave the room. Then the king said to the young man, "I know you are looking for your wife. But can you tell me what marks she has on her body?"

The young man replied, "Of course. I know her very well. There is a black spot on her breast."

The king undid her shirt and asked, "Look! Is this the mark?"

The man looked straight at her, and cried, "Oh! How . . ." The king made a gesture. "Be quiet. I'm going to release you. Tomorrow you must dress up as a lady and go to an eating house."

The king let the young man go. "That settles that case," she said to her minister. He was afraid to ask her what she meant.

Next day, the king went for a walk with her ministers. Suddenly the king stopped at the entrance to an eating house. There was a young lady at a table. The king looked at her for quite a long time, motionless. Then turning to the ministers, the king said, "Did you not want me to get married? Now I want you to know that I've found the young lady for me. She is now eating inside there. She is a good girl. I wish I were married to her."

When the ministers heard this, they all offered their congratulations. The marriage was settled without the least trouble. As for the wedding, it was as grand as could be.

When they were married, the king taught her husband every day how to handle affairs of state. She gave him some king's clothes to wear, to see how they felt. She taught him how to speak and walk like a real king. Gradually he learned everything. Soon he was good enough to appear in public. Then she said to him, "It's not good to keep up this lie. What's the use of pretending? Let's call a meeting of our people and let them know our secret. It's high time to decide how to punish those men I put in prison."

Next day all the gossip of the court was about the

king's face. It was so changed. Most people thought he must be seriously ill. As they whispered to each other, a palace gong sounded many times. It was the special signal for the whole city to gather together. So the chief minister, and the lesser ministers, the workers and the wastrels all hurried to the main gate of the palace. The whole city was there. After a short time, the king appeared. He was very changed. Beside him was his wife. She too was very changed. Not until the girl began to tell them the story of her past sufferings, in the familiar voice of the king, did the people realize what had happened.

The people were moved to tears by her pain. They clamoured to punish the wrong-doers. But the girl who had been king declared, "Let the gamblers go. They wouldn't have done anything wrong if I had not fallen into their hands. A spell in prison was quite enough. The four hunters are just common people. There couldn't be any grudge between us. So just let them go. But as for that so-called 'king', let's keep him in prison for ever and ever, lest he do harm to our ladies and young girls."

The Princess's Veil

It happened quite a long time ago. The king had a daughter, Billkis, whom he loved very dearly. Billkis was very beautiful and also very wise.

Billkis loved to be busy. She was especially good at embroidery. At the age of eight, she began to embroider her bridal veil with silk thread made by five thousand silkworms. The shuttle she used was carved by five thousand carpenters.

When she was sixteen, her special veil was ready. So the king decided to find her a husband. First he called together all the ministers of the court for her to choose among them, but she didn't like any of them.

"My dear daughter, who *do* you want?" the king asked worriedly.

The princess answered. "I only want the person who understands what my veil means. I don't care what kind of person he is, as long as he understands my veil; because then he will know what I am thinking."

75

The king didn't know what to do. He issued a proclamation, saying that no matter if he was a minister of the highest position or just an ordinary man, whoever could explain the princess's veil would marry her.

This message was hung up beside the veil on the palace walls. The news set the whole country a-buzz. For days people streamed to see the veil. Every man thought he had a chance of great happiness. Many came from a long way off, but they all went home disappointed. They could see it was a veil, but what thoughts were embroidered on it they could not tell.

Half a year passed. The king grew more and more anxious. He said, "Oh, my good daughter. Nobody can explain what your veil means. How could a stranger answer this riddle when even I, your father, am unable to guess what you are thinking about?"

"Dear father," the princess replied politely, "my inner thoughts are on the veil, for him to see who can."

Ten days later, at midnight, a ragged young man arrived from the east. He took down the veil and studied its pictures for a while. Then he walked into the palace.

The king was already in bed, but he got up again as soon as he heard somebody had taken down the veil without his permission. When they met, the king asked: "Can you read the veil? Do you know what the princess is thinking about? If you do not, you must go to gaol, because you took down the veil without asking me first."

"Most respected king," the young man said. "The pictures on the veil are the princess's thoughts. This I know." This was what the princess herself had said. The king called Billkis to meet the young man, and to question him.

Princess Billkis said, "What is on the veil?"

The young man answered, "There is a huge mountain on the veil. On the top of that mountain is a cave. Inside the cave is a green bird. Guarding the bird is a witch. The meaning is: "He who wins the green bird will win happiness.""

"You are perfectly right," said the princess. "Can you bring me that bird?"

"I would not have taken down the veil if I had no courage."

The king wasn't best pleased that this young upstart should win his daughter's love. But he asked, "Young man, do you want to try? I will supply all your needs."

The young man said, "I want nothing except the red pearl on the left side of the princess's head." The princess gave the pearl to him without hesitation. The young man took it and said goodbye.

After walking for three days and nights, he arrived at the huge mountain. He took out the red pearl and prayed, "My pearl! Everything depends on you. If you are not a false pearl, shine for me." Then he marched forward bravely. As he neared the cave, he could see the witch, sitting and snoring by the entrance.

The young man stopped at twenty paces. He took

the red pearl in his hand and held it out, then walked on. The witch heard his tread and jumped up. As she did, the red pearl sent out piercing red rays which forced the witch to close her eyes.

In no time at all the young man had run into the cave and snatched the green bird. He ran away while the witch was still shielding her eyes from the dazzling light of the pearl.

The young man took the green bird back to the palace. Handing it to the king, he said, "Now since I have brought you the precious bird, I'm going to ask you to let the princess go home with me."

The king thought for a while and said, "You are a man of great resource. Getting this bird was too easy a test. I'd like you to do something more. You'll marry her if you do well." Really, the king thought him a poor fellow and thought the princess would be well rid of him.

"All right, my dear king. You are welcome to make me do more," was the young man's brisk reply.

"There are fifty sludgy, stagnant pools in my palace grounds. I want you to clean them up so you can see the bottom, before tomorrow's Morning Prayer Ceremony, and fetch me a pail of clear water from each pond. That's all."

The young man agreed, and went into the palace garden. He looked at all the ponds, and found they were indeed as filthy as the king said. He sat down to think what to do.

Just then the princess came up to him, and said, "There's no need to worry or fear." She took a green

pearl from the right side of her head, and told him, "Take this pearl and dip it in each pond. The dirty water will become pure and clean."

The young man took it happily and started to clean the ponds with the green pearl.

At dawn, the young man took the king fifty pails of pure water from the ponds, and asked him to do as he had promised.

The king thought and thought, and finally said, "The grapes in my garden are not yet ripe but I wish I could eat them right now. I have a roll of silk which I want made into a jacket without using a single thread. I have one hundred servant girls in the palace; I'd like them to turn into men. My beard is growing longer and longer, but I wish I were as young as you. You must do all this within three days or I'll cut off your head."

The young man went out without a word. Princess Billkis said, "It's time for us to go!" So they took the veil and the green bird and rode away.

The king pursued them with his army, and caught them after a hundred miles. The king said, "My dear daughter, how cruel you are to leave your father and follow a good-for-nothing. Come home with me. I can find you an honourable husband." He ordered his soldiers to take the young man prisoner.

Princess Billkis set the green bird on the ground between the soldiers and the young man. Then she said to the king, "The saddest thing in the world is not the separation between us, but the breaking of promises again and again." The princess and the young man mounted on the green bird's back, and flew high into the sky. The king ordered the soldiers to shoot them down, but the princess unfolded her veil and hid them from sight.

People say that the young man and the Princess Billkis lived happily ever after. I've never heard tell otherwise.

The King and a Poor Man

Once there was a wise but poor old man who had an only son.

When the son grew up and left home, the old man didn't have anything to give him but advice. This is what he said: "Don't make friends with clever people, never borrow money from the newly rich, and never tell a secret even to your own wife. Take these instructions to heart, and keep them in mind under all circumstances."

The son pondered his father's words, and turned them over in his mind. He often thought to test whether his father was right or wrong. So he made a clever friend. He borrowed money from a man who had just become rich. And when his wife was out of the house, he killed a sheep and spilled its blood on his clothes. When his wife came home, he told her, "Wash the blood off my clothes. I killed a man." He added in a low voice, "I have told only you. I'll be for it if anyone finds out. It's a secret. Never refer to it again."

"You should know me by now," said his wife.

But not long after that, the couple had a fight. So the wife went straight to the king, and told him, "My husband has killed a man." The king gave orders for his immediate arrest.

On the way to court, the poor old man's son met his clever friend. "You'll stand by me, won't you?" he asked. But though the clever friend knew quite well he had killed only a sheep, and not a man, he didn't want to get involved. So he said, "I'm much too busy. If only I had the time to come to court . . . but, my hands are full." Then the poor man's son met the rich man who had recently lent him money. He told the rich man all about the case. The rich man thought to himself, "How can I get my money back if the king puts him in jail? The money I lent will be lost." So for fear he would not return the money later, the poor man's son was forced to give it back then and there.

At last he was brought to the king. He told the king all about his father's advice, and how he put it to the test. On hearing his story, the king decided that the man's poor father was the wisest man on earth. He obviously knew almost everything there was to know. And the son was no fool. He let the son go free, and thought often after that of the good sense the son had shown, and the good advice the father had given.

He thought so much, in fact, that he couldn't sleep. He thought, they are stronger than I am. They know more than I do. Much more. What could I do if they decided to seize my crown?

Finally, he closed his mind to mercy and determined to have them killed. He had them buried alive, father and son.

The very next day the king took ill. A little bit of bone got stuck in his throat. All the fashionable doctors were consulted, but none of them could get the bone out. Finally one of the ministers grouped round the king's bed said, "O respected king, why did you order us to bury that poor father and son? Perhaps they could have made you better, if they were still alive. Then you wouldn't be in such pain."

The king felt quite differently about the father and son today. He said, "Maybe they are still alive. Hurry up and dig them out, and bring them to me."

They were still alive. Just as they were thrust into the hole, the poor old man had held a bamboo cane aloft, and they had managed to breathe through that, and to keep up their strength they had eaten a little sour cream which the old man had been carrying. But they were very angry, and though they were happy to be let out of the hole, they would not go to the king. "We are not going to do anything for that king," they said. "He had no reason to have us buried."

The king was helpless. He thought he must die soon. He sent his ministers to ask for help again and again. He promised to give up his crown and all his property if only the dangerous bone in his throat could be taken out and he was freed of pain.

At that, the father and son had to go to him. The king begged their pardon for burying them alive, and asked them to take out the bone. The poor man said,

"O mighty king, it is not hard to ease your trouble, but you must pay a great price. You must kill your only son."

The king didn't want to do that. But all the ministers said he should. They said, "You are the king. It is worth anything to save your life."

Finally the king agreed.

Fearfully, the king watched them tie his son up. The poor man picked up a cleaver. The king's son was on the brink of death. The king looked even sicker than before. The poor man waved his cleaver and said, "Bring a screen right away. Don't let the king watch this."

The king couldn't see behind the screen, but he could hear. A desperate yell rang out. The king couldn't help crying out at the top of his voice. And the shudder of that cry shook his throat so hard that the little bit of bone slipped out.

Then the poor man told the king that he had killed only a sheep, not a man. The king's son was alive and well.

The king was so relieved that he kept his promise, and gave up his crown and all his riches to the poor man and the poor man's son.

The Story of Washing Horse Pond

One of the most beautiful of Dali's nineteen peaks is called the Treasure Peak. There is a clean pond at the top of the peak, from which pure water flows all the year round. It is surrounded by trees and flowers, and is known as Washing Horse Pond. Next to the pond stands a large stone about the size of a man. People say that this stone is the statue of the brave young man who was called Akui, a long long time ago.

Once in Dali there was a terrible drought. For three whole years there had not been a single drop of rain. All the pools and ditches had dried up. Even huge Dali Lake had lost its fresh colour and shrunk to a muddy puddle. There were no more azaleas on the mountain slopes, and no birds sang. The crops wouldn't grow and the cattle wouldn't thrive. All the beautiful mountains were sadly changed. People lived in despair.

Under one of those nineteen peaks, in the village of

Boluo, there lived a young man by the name of Akui. His parents were old and weak. Because of the three years' drought, they could harvest nothing. Akui was forced to scrape a living by looking for firewood in the hills. His parents just got older and weaker. A doctor was called, but there was nothing he could do. It was the drought. Many people could do nothing except wait to die. Akui's parents had no money to buy medicine or food. Very soon they died, one after the other. Akui was very sad.

All the neighbours came to pay their respects. They too were suffering. Some of the old men talked of an unfailing spring that was supposed to be somewhere at the top of the mountain peaks, but none of them knew where. Akui made up his mind to go to seek that spring. He took a hoe, a bow and arrows, and some food, and set off first for the peak above the village. The villagers watched him go, and all their hopes and worries went with him.

For nine days and ten nights he climbed, over four huge peaks and four dried-up river beds, till he reached the top of the highest peak, the Peak of Horses and Dragons. After his long journey Akui was so tired that he fell asleep as soon as he lay down.

The day was just dawning when he awoke. As he looked around, all he could see was dry grass and withered trees. There was no water in the streams. There was no water anywhere. He searched all day, but found nothing. That night he could not sleep. He just stared at the sky all night. And suddenly, he saw something shining in the dark sky away to the south.

The shining thing passed over his head and landed on another peak. Akui was astonished at the sight, and set out straight away for the other peak.

Dawn had come when Akui got there. Looking all around, he found everything just as dried up as everywhere else. Except for one pine tree under a large rock. Its branches were green, and the needles were lush. Akui thought: Water! A tree lives on water. There must be water underneath the tree.

Lifting his hoe, he dug furiously till late that night. He dug till his hands were stained with blood, and his parched lips split with effort. His throat was a burning fire. And still he found no trace of water.

That evening, to be safe from wild beasts, Akui climbed up the tree. He was so tired after digging all day that he soon fell asleep. At midnight he was woken by a sudden flash of light. Looking up in the sky he saw a number of winged horses flying to the large rock. The leading horse was as white as snow, and larger than the rest. It stretched out its leg and struck the rock three times, and the rock opened, just like a gate. And within was a real pond of pure water.

The flying horses drank and splashed. They didn't leave until day was about to break. The rock closed again behind them.

Akui jumped down from the tree and ran towards the rock. He hit it three times with his hoe. Slowly, the stone gate opened. He went inside, and found a lovely pool of rippling water. Grass and flowers grew on its banks. On a stone were carved the words "Washing Horse Pond".

Akui knelt to drink. It tasted very cool. He was too excited to drink as much as he wished to. He was thinking of his fellow villagers. They were relying on him in their hour of need. They were suffering. So he started to dig a channel straight away.

In a wink, a stream of white smoke issued from the ground, and in front of Akui stood a white-haired old man, who said, "Young man, this water must not be touched. This is the only pond where the flying horses come to drink and swim. I am the God of this mountain peak, and this pond is in my care."

Akui told him all about the misery caused by the drought. He told him of the people's suffering. As he told the god about the death of his parents, he couldn't keep back his tears.

The God of Treasure Peak was very much moved by Akui's true story. He said, "Young fellow, let me tell you the truth. The one who frees the water of this magic pond will turn into a piece of rock. So young as you are now, don't you think it a pity to become a stone? Go down and tell them to send up an old man instead. It is too much. It is more than enough for you to have found the water for everybody."

Akui hesitated for a while after hearing this. He replied, "My respected uncle, I thank you for your kindness. But there must be no delay. This water will save thousands of lives. I'd rather be stone than go back now. You needn't worry about me."

He began to dig again.

Soon Akui had dug out a channel, down which the pure water rushed. All along its path, the trees began to shoot green leaves, the birds sang, and all the mountain flowers came into bloom.

Akui shouted for joy. He tried to walk out and watch the world come back to life, but alas! he couldn't find his feet. Looking down, he saw his two feet had turned into a pair of stone feet. He tried to shout aloud, but his lungs were turned to stone lungs. All his body was turning to stone. Akui knew now he could never return to his village; but he heard the water gurgling by, and knew it would go there for him. He was content. He let his mouth set into a happy loving stone smile.

The villagers were full of joy when the water from Washing Horse Pond reached them. The once dry plain was turning green as the water passed. Everyone knew Akui must have found the water. They climbed up to the pond to look for him, but where had he gone? They couldn't find even Akui's shadow. They called and called at the tops of their voices but nobody answered. Finally, they noticed the standing stone. The more they looked at it, the more it looked like Akui. A hoe was lying by, with mossy grass still sticking to it. From this more than anything, the people knew that Akui had indeed become a stone image.

From that time on, men and women from the villages down on the plain often came up to visit Akui, the hero who had given up his life for them. They made Washing Horse Pond a place of beauty, and it still is. Camellias are everywhere. The trees are thick and green, and the smell of the flowers is exquisite. It is said that the ancient kings of Dali used to spend their summer days by its banks. And even now, Akui stands stone still beside the precious water.

A Crane and Two Brothers

Once upon a time there lived two farmers who were brothers. The elder brother was very cruel and loved money very much. He wanted to get more and more, no matter what he had to do. When they divided their inheritance, the selfish elder brother gave the younger brother only a knife and a broken basket. The younger brother was an honest man, kind to his friends and fair to his neighbours. He thought the division was mean, but he didn't complain.

In order to earn a living, the young brother had to get busy looking for firewood with his knife and basket.

One day after breakfast the young brother went to cut wood as usual. After climbing to the top of a mountain, he sat down for a rest. Suddenly a large crane came and stood just next to him.

"What are you doing here alone?" the crane asked.

The young brother was surprised to hear a crane talk, so he replied, "I am very poor. There is nothing

to eat. I come here to look for firewood so that I can sell it and buy something to eat."

The crane asked, "Is this true or false?"

"I am telling you the truth," the young brother replied. "It's perfectly true."

The crane then said, "If that's the case, I'll help you. Now listen to me. I'll take you to gather gold at the Sun Mountain. But be sure to remember this: you must take away only one nugget. No more."

The young brother nodded. "I'll do as you say."

The crane took him on its back. They flew up in the air and very soon they arrived at the Sun Mountain. It was early in the afternoon, but on that strange mountain the sun was about to set. Looking round, the young brother could see nothing but gold. The whole mountain was littered with shining gold. As the crane had told him, he picked up only one nugget, before they flew back to their starting place.

Delightedly fingering the gold in his pocket, the younger brother returned to his home. He sold the gold and bought some pigs, some cows, some horses, and many many other things. He bought new clothes, and grain, and farm tools. In short, he supplied all his needs.

His greedy brother couldn't believe the change. "Where did you get all these things?" he asked.

The young one told him the truth. "I gathered gold at the Sun Mountain."

His brother sneered, "Where is this so-called Sun Mountain, and how did you get there?"

The young man said, "I was taken to the place by a

big crane." And he told his brother the story from beginning to end.

The next day, the elder brother did just as the young one had done before. He got a knife, a basket, and a large bag. He went to the place where his brother used to cut wood. As he sat down to rest, the crane came from the sky. The crane landed next to him, and asked, "What are you doing here alone?"

He said hurriedly, "I am very poor. There is nothing to eat. I come here to look for firewood so that I can sell it and buy something to eat."

The crane asked, "Is this true or false?"

The elder brother answered eagerly, "Really I'm poor. Very very poor indeed."

The crane said, "If that's the case, I'll take you to gather gold at the Sun Mountain, but remember what I say. You must take only one nugget."

The elder brother nodded in agreement.

Then the crane carried him on his back to the Sun Mountain. The sun there had already gone down.

The elder brother saw that the whole mountain was covered in yellow gold. He took no notice of the crane's warning. He filled his basket first. That wasn't enough. Then he filled his bag. Then he filled his pockets. At last he had all he could carry, and turned to go, but there and then the sun rose. In less than a minute he was burnt to death between the golden sun and the golden mountain.

A Stone Sheep

At Dayao county in Western Yunnan, there is a commune known as Stone Sheep Commune. The peasants there are mostly of the Yi nationality. Salt is their main product, and the famous salt mine was named after a stone sheep. This is the story.

No one knows exactly when it was, but once the Dragon King of Dongting Lake had a little daughter. She was sharp-witted, and brave, and as pretty as a camellia. One beautiful day, the sun was shining warm on the waters of the lake, and in the fishing boats all the fishermen were singing. The Dragon King's daughter was attracted to the lake by their song. Led by a little chambermaid, she secretly came out to play along the bank.

Now it so happened that the Dragon King of Dali Lake was passing by and saw her. He fell in love with her at first sight, for she was really so charming. He wanted her to come with him. At first, he asked her in

a polite manner. She showed no willingness. In the end, she was taken to Dali Lake by force. Upon their arrival, he tried to bully her into marrying him.

The daughter of the Dragon King of Dongting Lake was a noble and upright girl. No matter what, she would never give in. The Dragon King of Dali Lake was so angry, he sent her to look after a flock of three hundred sheep in a deep valley. She was not allowed to return unless she agreed to marry him.

The poor girl drove the sheep along the valley for many days. She drank cold water when she was thirsty, and when she felt hungry she could eat only wild fruit. She walked barefoot, and slept under bushes.

The girl drove the sheep to the mountain area where the Yi people lived. That year, as a result of the callous behaviour of the Dragon King of Dali Lake, there was a drought. The plants were parched. The animals were dying of thirst. Fire was seen in the mountains.

The Yi people were very poor; too poor even to afford salt. Now that the Dragon King was too lazy to make rain, things were desperate. There was no water and little food. Two hundred of the girl's sheep died. She made up her mind to seek water so that the Yi people could live.

She climbed over ninety-nine hilltops and ninety-nine rocky peaks. Her feet were seriously pierced by stings. Where her blood fell, camellias in full bloom shot up. Where her sweat fell, there grew the grass people call "good for everything".

She walked until she came to the Dragon King of Dali Lake's own spring, sealed up with the Dragon King's stone seal. When her tears fell on the stone, the seal cracked open, and water gushed out to irrigate the whole area. The Yi people were saved. The whole earth seemed to change. The buckwheat turned green. The girl scattered the dung of her sheep onto the buckwheat, and soon there was a fine harvest.

The Yi villagers loved her. Tenderly, they called her "Sheep Maiden". The village girls gave her their best skirts. The young men sang beautiful songs and played lovely tunes to her. The children all offered to help look after her sheep.

But though the drought was over, the villagers still had no salt of their own. So the Sheep Maiden just said, "Thank you, I cannot stay," and, driving her sheep ahead, set off on another journey to seek salt for them.

Once again the Sheep Maiden climbed over ninety-nine hilltops and ninety-nine rocky peaks. Her sheep-skin coat was torn to pieces. Her skirt was almost a useless rag. She dragged on, step by step, over rocks and stones. Thirty-three sheep fell to their deaths, but still she found no salt. Her food was gone, her eyes were aching all the time, but still she kept on looking, and still she found no salt. Another thirty-three sheep died of tiredness. Another thirty-three were ravaged by tigers and wolves. Still she found no salt. Now there was only one sheep left. Worn out with wounds, with hunger and with thirst, she was too tired to go on. She fell asleep under a rock.

When she was woken by a cool breeze, her last sheep was missing. She set out at once to find it. From down the slope she heard a bleat, and in spite of her sores she rushed towards it. She found her last white sheep pushing fiercely into the ground, head first. Half of its body was under the ground. The girl seized the sheep by the tail. The tail came in two, but the sheep didn't stop pushing. What was to be done?

Then she thought: perhaps there is a salt mine under the ground. Sheep like salt; everyone knows that. She picked up some soil, and found it very salty. Oh, salt was hidden there! The Sheep Maiden was so excited that she lay down on the ground and started digging with her bare hands. Her ten fingers were splitting, her blood mixing with the soil. Finally, a vein of salt appeared.

A long time passed, but the Sheep Maiden didn't return to the villages. How people wished to see her again! At last, a group of young men took their knives and rifles and set out to find the girl. When they reached the salt mine, they found the Sheep Maiden's body. Her hands were buried in the ground. The white sheep next to her had turned to stone.

From that time on, the Yi people had no trouble getting salt. They called the mine, "Temple of the Dragon Daughter". Inside the temple, there was a picture of the Dragon Daughter, but she was dressed as a Sheep Maiden, in the style of the local Yi girls.

A Golden Fish

Quite a long time ago, there was a man whose family lived by catching fish. One day he caught in his net a fish of pure gold. Of course, he was excited, and as happy as could be, but just as he stretched out his hand to take it, the fish leapt and freed itself into the river again. The fisherman felt so sad that he trudged off home with a picture of the golden fish stuck in his mind. After that he fished there everyday, and caught as many fish as he wanted, but never the golden one.

He lived by fishing for three years and earned a lot of money. So he changed his occupation and set up shop as a cloth merchant. But however much his life improved, he could never forget that shining fish.

It happened that the man's wife died, and he married another woman who already had a son. In the beginning, he loved this step-son, but it didn't last long. He kept thinking that the boy wasn't his own son, and grew to dislike him. Moreover, he was often away from home on business, and had little time for the boy.

One day, the boy saw somebody fishing along the riverside. Remembering that there was a fishing net in their house, he hurried home and said to his mother, "Let me have that net and I'll catch some fish for you."

His mother told him, "No, you are too young to fish in the river." But the boy wouldn't listen to her. Finally she gave in and let him take the net.

The boy fished with his net. After a little while, he lifted it from the water and found there was a golden fish in it. Quickly he grabbed hold of it, and in another moment he had set off for home. As he walked, he thought: Shall I sell it or cook it at home? He looked at it carefully, and thought it would be sad to eat it. He said out loud, "It's a bad thing to eat such a wonderful fish. After all it is much better for you to live freely in the river." He turned back to the river, set the fish free, and returned home with an empty net.

Some boys saw this, and ran to tell his stepfather at the shop. "We saw your son catch a fish as yellow as gold, but the funny boy threw it back in the river again."

The merchant was furious to hear this. He thought: I've brooded about that golden fish for eight years. And now he's thrown it away. I would be a millionaire if I had that fish.

He was so annoyed that he ran home with a dagger in his hand. Seizing the boy, he asked him, "Who told you to let my golden fish go?"

The boy was so frightened he stood stock still and

grew dumb. The merchant got angrier still. Pointing his dagger at the boy's breast, he shouted, "To me, a golden fish is much more precious than a silly boy like you."

The mother cried out to stop him. "How cruel you are to kill him for nothing but a fish!" She begged again and again, but all in vain. Finally she said, "Well, you must not kill him in daytime. If you insist on killing the boy, do it in the dark so that people won't know." The merchant agreed to this and left.

The mother and son hugged and sobbed. She said: "My boy, you mustn't stay here. Go away from me!" Then she prepared a bag of cakes for him, and told him, "Remember what I'm telling you now. If you meet someone and want them to be your travelling companion, go a little way with them and then say, 'I need to squat. Wait for me.' If the man waits for you, make him a good friend. If he doesn't wait, you needn't bother with him any more." Again they embraced, and said goodbye to each other.

As he walked, the boy met a man who accompanied him for half a day. He thought of his mother's words and said, "Sorry, I need to squat. Wait for me."

The man stood for a little while and then said, "I'll walk ahead." The man left him, and the boy thought, "What my mother told me was right." He walked on and on.

On the way he met another man, and the same thing happened when he tried to test him. But on the third day, as the sun was setting, a tall strong young man appeared suddenly at his right side. This young man said, "Hello! My young brother, let's walk together. Why are you alone?"

The boy honestly told him the facts. "My father wanted to kill me for setting free a golden fish. My mother helped me escape. I don't know where I should go."

The young man comforted him. "Don't worry. We shall stay together wherever we go. I'll help you tackle everything."

The boy tested the stranger as his mother had told him, and this time the stranger waited for him. From that time they walked together like a pair of brothers.

After two days' journey they arrived at a big town. Here the people had a custom that anyone who ate food without paying for it would be sentenced to death. Naturally, the two newcomers knew nothing about this local law. Wandering about the street, they felt very hungry when they saw food on sale.

The boy said, "Our pockets are empty. I wish we could eat something."

The young man said, "Why not? We can work for our food instead of paying for it."

They entered a restaurant and ordered many bowls of noodles, and ate a lot of buns. When the time came to pay, they asked to work in the kitchen instead. But the manager said, "No," and reported them to the king.

The king said he would hear the case that evening. The two were tied up and brought before him.

The king asked, "You enjoyed eating their food, why did you not pay for it?"

They answered, "We are wanderers. There is no money in our pockets, but we are willing to work to make up for what we have eaten."

The king declared in a loud voice, "He who eats without paying is a cheat. He must be sentenced to death. That is my strict law. Take them out and hang them up on the gallows."

A minister said, "Your Majesty, might I have a word?"

The king answered, "I am listening."

"Those two young fellows are neither weak nor sick. They are strong and healthy. Seven years ago, a witch stole away your daughter. Those you sent to rescue her were all eaten. Now my suggestion is: let those lads have a go. If they succeed in rescuing your daughter, you can make them ministers and one of them can marry her. It wouldn't be too late to hang them if they fail. What do you think of that?"

The king agreed with this suggestion. They were called back at once. "My daughter was kidnapped by a witch. I'll give you both a surprising reward if you can succeed in rescuing her."

They stood up and boldly promised they would fulfill the mission.

The king gave them a magic fighting sword. Moreover, two of his own red horses were provided for them to ride. With such a splendid weapon, and such magnificent horses, they set out full of confidence.

Two days later their way was barred by a huge mountain. There was no path over its rocks. So they tied the horses at the bottom and began to climb. When they reached the crest, the young man asked the boy, "What do you see?"

"Brother, there is a golden building at the foot of the mountain. There is a river to its right, with a big bridge."

As they looked, the witch appeared. She cried out in a proud voice, "Who are you? How dare you come here! Are you looking for a place to die?" She opened her eyes as wide as bowls. Greedy water streamed out of her wide gaping mouth. It looked as though she would swallow them up with one gulp.

The two young men were not afraid at all. They pulled out their sword.

The witch swaggered about her power. "Only two. Come a hundred or a thousand like you, they are doomed to be eaten here. Have you heard of my great power? Your king has sent thousands of soldiers here, and I just draw breath to take off their skins. Their bones are blown up in the air. The mountain top you are standing on was piled up with nothing but bones. Little sonnies, both of you are just like babies, too young to do anything. I will draw a breath and your bodies will make a tasty snack for me."

Before the witch had finished her boasting, the young boy had begun to point the magic sword at her. Seeing this, the tall strong young man called out, "Young brother, take care! Leave this to me."

The witch laughed. "Good. You want to die first."

As she said this, she drew a great rasping breath. The boy let go of the long sword. Sucked in by the strong whirlwind of her breath, the boy's sword danced into the witch's throat. Her head was split into two halves on the instant. Her blood gushed out like running water in a river.

The two companions had won the battle. As they cleaned the blood from the long sword, a beautiful girl came out of the golden building, with a golden kettle in her hand. She bowed down politely as she caught sight of them. "Hello, young men. Where did you two come from? Don't you know ordinary people aren't allowed to come here?"

"The king's princess was stolen away," they answered. "We have come to look for her."

"You will die if the witch sees you. Go away at once. I am the king's daughter. Go. Thousands of soldiers sent by my father to rescue me have all been eaten."

They replied, "Well princess, just go and have a look over there."

The princess saw the dead body of the witch. She could hardly believe it. "You have put an end to the witch! You are heroes. But I must tell you she has two sons. They have been gone for forty days, and are due back home today."

"Princess don't be afraid. You needn't worry. We can deal with them," they answered.

The two brothers went into the golden building and a grand feast was served. Then the young man stood in front of the building, to protect the princess, and the boy hid himself beneath the bridge, to wait for the return of the witch's two sons.

Soon the witch's sons, the White Wizard and the Black Wizard, came home. Even in the distance, they could smell something unusual. Snuff, snuff. "I smell the blood of a mortal man. Come out, come out, as quick as you can."

The boy jumped out. "You wicked wizards! We have come to get the king's daughter back. If you don't give in, I'll tear your bellies into pieces and cut off your heads."

"You talk like a child who was just born yesterday," the White Wizard sneered. "How you boast. You are seeking to die." Saying this, he held up his great spear, thirty metres long, and aimed it at the boy's heart.

The boy was brave. He struck the spear with his sword and it snapped in two. The Black Wizard took fright. He thought: That was my brother's unbreakable spear with which he lifted up the famous Kunlun mountain. How fierce this sonny is! I must teach him some manners.

The Black Wizard was like a maddened bear. He lifted his one ton hammer and swung it at the boy. The boy didn't alter his quiet easy bearing. He gave the hammer a light touch with his magic sword. The iron hammer broke into two halves and fell to the ground. The boy sheathed his sword. Then he lifted the two wizards high in his hands, and dashed them to the ground. The White Wizard and the Black Wizard were killed with one stroke of his magic sword. Their two heads were hung on the bridge.

The young man ran from the house to embrace the boy. They found their horses and took the princess home. They rode over plains, deserts and wastelands. At last they rested in a village near the king's palace, where many people came out to welcome them. A white-haired old man went to report their arrival to the king. The king thought he must be dreaming.

"You may cut off my head if this news is false," said the old man, running his fingers through his moustache. So the king gave him a plateful of gold coins. Then, gathering up his ministers and four hundred soldiers, all playing various musical instruments, the king marched to the village. The ministers then carried the heroes in glory back to the palace.

After seven days the minister who had advised the king to send them against the witch brought the young men a message from the king. "I shall be very glad to let one of these young men marry my daughter if he is willing to do so."

Well, both of them couldn't say "Yes."

Finally the elder one said, "It is better for you to marry her. I cannot get married. You will find out why later." The boy agreed, and the decision was reported to the king.

The king arranged the wedding, and they were married, and very happy they were.

Another week passed. On the eighth day, the young man said, "My little brother, I must be off home. You can stay here."

"If you leave, I'll follow. I'm not willing to stay here without you."

The king heard this, and begged them to stay forever, but no matter how he pleaded, they would not listen. The king had to let his daughter go. Before they left, he filled bags with grain, silver and gold for them.

They walked a long long way. One day, as they were passing a wide river, the young man told them to stop. He asked the boy; "What did you get when you cast your net into this river at the age of fifteen?"

"I caught a golden fish," the boy replied.

"What did you do with that fish?"

"I threw the fish back into the river again."

"My brother, you are a kind-hearted boy. I am that golden fish. How kind you were to let me go. It was you who gave me life. You threw me back. You suffered a great deal, all because of me. That's why I returned to reward you. That's all I want to say. Goodbye."

When he had finished speaking he dived into the river. In a little while, a shining golden fish swam to the surface. He put his head out of the water to say "Goodbye" and disappeared.

The Two Brothers

Once there were two brothers. The elder one was very handsome, but the younger one was a plain boy. Their mother loved only her handsome son. She gave him good things to eat and new clothes to wear. The young one ate scraps and dressed in rags. Furthermore, the younger one had to plough the field as well as gather firewood up in the mountains.

Yet though the elder brother enjoyed all the best things, and wore clothes of the best quality, he looked pale and weak. Meanwhile his brother who was badly treated looked healthy and seemed tireless all the year round. When they were grown, their mother made a division between them. The elder one got all the best land and a big strong ox; the younger had to make do with a small rocky plot and a little black dog. The dog was too small to do anything but follow at his heels; that's why his mother let him have it.

For all this ill treatment, the younger one didn't feel sorry for himself. Leading his little black dog, he

moved to his rocky patch of mountain and built a cottage there. So he didn't have an ox? Well, he had his own way of managing things. He cut down a tree to make a plough and tied it to the dog. Then he scattered lots of pieces of bun on the ground. The dog would drag the plough a little, eat some bun, then totter a few steps more. That way, they ploughed the whole plot. The young brother knew just how to farm. He dug the soil deeply and planted his seeds very carefully. He worked hard, and got a bumper harvest. All his boxes and all his bags were filled with grain.

The elder brother had been spoilt by his doting mother, so he looked down on work. He just liked to eat and play. In the end, his crops were the worst in the whole district.

"What is the matter with me?" he asked himself. He decided, "The main reason must be the dog. My ox is much bigger but it is useless. He has a dog. That's why he does so well and I get such thin crops." So one day he asked the young one, "May I borrow your black dog to plough my field?"

The young one lent the dog with pleasure. The elder brother scattered buns on the ground, but the black dog wouldn't move. The brother got angry, and killed the dog with a long knife. For many days the younger brother waited for his favourite dog to return, but in vain. He went to his brother's house, and learned that his dog had been killed. He took the dog home, and buried him sadly in front of his cottage.

The following year, green bamboo trees grew from the dog's grave. When the young brother shook the trees, money fell down from them. The elder one was furious when he learned of this good luck. One day, sneaking up while his brother was out, he secretly shook the bamboo trees. But instead of money, a shower of dog's droppings fell down on his head.

He got angry again, and cut down the bamboo trees. The younger brother was very sad. He collected their branches, and buried them in the ground. And where he had buried them, there soon grew some winter melon plants. That year he had a great crop of winter melons, but wicked monkeys used to come and damage them. So he made a plan. He emptied the seeds from the largest melon, and then hid himself inside it to keep guard.

Despite himself, he fell asleep. When he woke up, he was not on his own plot. He had been carried away to the foot of a big rock. There were a great number of monkeys jostling and chattering. An owl was reciting some holy scriptures. In front of the winter melon the monkeys had piled up golden bowls and jade dishes. They were worshipping the melon. They were pretending it was a pig, and getting ready to kill it as an offering to their god. The young brother decided enough was enough. He jumped out of the melon with a loud shout. The owl flew off, and the terrified monkeys scattered in all directions. The young brother loaded himself with all the gold and jade and went home.

When the news reached the elder brother's ears, his

hatred was beyond description. One day, he secretly went to the younger brother's melon plot. Copying his brother's idea, he scooped out a melon and hid in it to wait for the monkeys to take him. Soon, his wish was fulfilled. The monkeys all pulled together and lugged the melon to the top of a high mountain. This time there were no jade or golden dishes. There was no owl, no worshipping or anything else. When the monkeys arrived at the top, they just pushed the melon down from a rock. The melon rolled down, thump, thump, *crash*, and so did the brother, and that was the end of him.

After that, the owl came back. All the monkeys were pleased with a good job done. They all sang and danced, as happy as could be.

Green Dragon Pond

In a valley below a peak by the name of Malong in Dali there is a pure, still pond, like a roll of white cloth. This pond is neither big nor small. You think you can see the bottom. It looks no deeper than a man's leg. But the instant you enter that pond, ice-cold water will reach up to your waist. In another minute you will be nowhere to be seen. Not long ago some brave foolish boys went in for a dare, and they never came back. This is the famous Green Dragon Pond – an uncanny place, where a dragon might really live.

It is said that once there did live in this pond a dragon who could change himself into a man. From the very beginning to the end, this dragon did no harm, but only good deeds. For this reason, the villagers around Malong peak lived a happy life. The rain came when needed, and there weren't any disastrous storms or other catastrophes. From year to year they worked peacefully and harvested all they needed and more.

To the side of the pond there was a grand temple, in

which lived an old monk and his two novices. This old monk knew a great deal about Buddha and could recite many holy scriptures. But his chief interest was chess: he was a master player. He would scour the neighbourhood for strangers to play against, but always ended up disappointed, because his opponents knew so little. His hopes were always dashed. Again and again he grumbled to himself, because he couldn't find a worthy opponent at chess.

One windy, rainy afternoon, a very handsome, beautifully dressed young fellow walked in through the temple gate. His brow shone, and his eyes were clear and deep. He made a polite bow as he entered. "Greetings, respected master."

The old monk asked, "Where are you from and what blows you into my temple?"

"Dear master, my name is Li Aiqi. I live in a village down the valley. Well, I was on my way to the hills for a walk, but an unexpected downpour forced me to trouble you for shelter, just for a little while, here in your grand temple."

On hearing this, the old monk said warmly, "Most rare and precious guest, please come into my sitting-room and rest yourself. Just wait for my pupils to bring you a cup of tea."

The old monk's sitting room was spotlessly clean and tidy. The walls were hung with landscape pictures and Buddhist texts. In the centre of the room was a splendid marble table, and on the table was a chess-board. Really, it was a very pleasant room of the old monk's. The young man entered, and looked around. His eyes were held by the chess-board. He just stared at it, fascinated. The old monk noticed, and asked joyfully, "You don't play chess, do you?"

"Yes master, I like it, but I am not very good at it."

"Oh, don't say that. Come on. Let's try a game right now."

All the while muttering that he really wasn't very good, the young fellow sat down and began to play with great concentration. At first the old monk was confident, and didn't pay much attention. He just made the logical moves, and watched the game turn out as he expected. Then, all of a sudden, he lost an important piece. He couldn't understand it. How could such a thing happen? In no time at all, two more chessmen were lost, one after another. The old monk began to worry. He realized he dared not underestimate this young fellow. He concentrated his thoughts and paid close attention to every move. It grew late, and still their game was unfinished. They played and played, and it was hard to say who was winning. At last, it was too dark to carry on. The old monk knew he had finally met his match, and the young man seemed to be enjoying it too, but he stood up and said, "Master, I'm sorry to say I must be off home now."

The old monk was getting more and more involved in the game, and said quickly, "Oh, it can't be time yet. Why don't you stay for the night? It is too dark to go. What is more, our game, as you see, is still . . ."

"Oh, as for the game, I promise to play and learn from you again tomorrow."

"Very well, tomorrow. We will play more tomorrow, but there's no need for you to go. Stay with us here."

"Master, I must get back, or my family will be anxious. I will come again tomorrow." So saying, the young man disappeared into the night.

Early the next day, the young fellow returned to the temple, and played many games with the old monk. They were an even match. After that they played chess all the time, day after day. They soon became firm friends. They liked each other so well, they could speak from heart to heart without any hesitation. It was as if they had known each other all their lives.

Time passed as swiftly as an arrow through the air. Half a year slipped by. Gradually the old monk began to wonder about Li Aiqi. "This fellow introduced himself as a man from a village, so how come he is always free to play chess? We monks are said to be very free people? Is there any person who is as free as a monk? And why must he always leave in the evening?" The old monk was greatly puzzled by these questions.

One day, as they were playing a game, the old man ventured to ask the young fellow, "Well Aiqi, tell me, exactly which village do you belong to? Why must you always go back there in the evening?"

The young man smiled, and said, "My old master, now let me tell you the truth. My home is not so far away. It is quite near your temple. We have been old neighbours for many years."

The old monk was very surprised. "I don't believe it. You, young man, will have your joke. Where is there another house round here?"

"My master, would I lie to you? I live right beside your temple. The Green Pond is my home."

"You live in the pond?" The old monk was even more astonished.

"That's right. In fact," said Li Aiqi, in a perfectly serious tone, "I'm not a man at all. I am a dragon."

"A dragon. Oh, come on. I don't believe it. I don't." The old monk shook his head.

"Master, if you don't believe me, just come to the pond and watch while I fetch something for you."

The old monk followed the young fellow to the pond, not believing a word. There the gloomy, ice-cold water was. Where was the bottom? The old monk shivered and took hold of the young man's hand. "Don't make fun of me. How can a pond of water be your home?"

The young man took back his hand, and dived into the pond like a well-trained swimmer. "My dear!" the old monk cried out, and stepped back. He dared not look, but he had to know. He stood on a rock and looked down into the pool. His body was trembling all over. Where was the young fellow? Aiqi was nowhere. Not even a trace of his shadow was to be seen. At first the old monk saw air bubbles coming to the surface, but they soon stopped. Now there was nothing. The old monk felt so sad. He wept bitterly. But just as he was about to call his two novices from the temple, he suddenly saw bubbles rising once more in the water. In another minute, the young fellow was standing in front of the monk, holding a silver plate in his hands. There was not a drop of water on his body. On the plate there was a beautiful monk's robe. Smiling, he told the old monk, "Most respected master, I've brought you a little gift. See if it fits."

The old monk was too excited to utter a word. He unfolded the robe then and there. It twinkled in all directions, and the whole valley seemed brighter and more beautiful than before. It really was a priceless treasure. The old monk folded it quickly and returned it. "I'm ashamed to accept it. I'm not worthy to receive and enjoy such a great treasure."

Li Aiqi said, "Of course for a monk this really is special. It's a magic robe and has been untold years in the treasury of my Dragon Palace. Now, to mark the friendship between us, I'm very happy to give it to you. One of these days you will find it invaluable."

The old monk couldn't refuse his sincere offer. He had to accept it. From that time on, their friendship deepened. With the exception of cloudy and rainy days, when the Green Dragon had to make rain, they always met and played chess. The Green Dragon would bring food from his Dragon Palace for the old monk to eat.

One day, the old monk said, "Dear Aiqi, now I believe you are a real out-and-out dragon. But everyone knows that a dragon is not a man. I don't understand why you look just like a man."

The Green Dragon smiled. "You are right. A

dragon ought to be quite different from a man. Listen: this is not my real shape!"

"It's a pity that I've never seen in all my life the shape of a dragon. My friend, will you show me your real body?"

That was a poser. The Green Dragon could only say, "Listen to me, master, it's impossible. An ordinary man is not allowed to see a true dragon. You would be terrified."

"But we are as close as family! Of course outsiders can't see, but our friendship is special. You must agree with me, Aiqi. Please let me see you once."

The Green Dragon shook his head, but the old monk was eager to see a real dragon, and begged time and again. Finally the Green Dragon was forced to say, "Master, you must understand my position. It isn't that I am not willing to show you. If a mortal man like you saw my real shape, I could never again become a man. All the good deeds I've been doing for thousands of years would be finished and gone. I should be good for nothing. Anything might happen."

"Oh. I never thought of that. But surely a Buddhist monk is allowed to see a dragon?"

"A monk is the same as an ordinary man. But in our case, there is a difference. For almost a year now we have been close friends. From time to time we've eaten magic fruits and handled enchanted things from the Dragon Palace. So, there is a chance. But it's hard to be certain."

On hearing this, the monk began to feel happy. He

thought his wish would come true. Therefore he begged more ardently. "You know we are not casual acquaintances, but very good friends. Show me today."

"Oh, no, no, we are not making fun. There are others in this temple, aren't there?" said the Green Dragon.

There really is hope, the old monk thought to himself. He said, "That is simple. Early tomorrow morning I'll send the novices to town for supplies. I'll tell them not to return until late in the afternoon. So there will be no third person inside or outside the temple. For extra safety, we can lock the gate. Nobody will know what we are doing." The Green Dragon was silent, so the old monk continued, "Dear friend, I'm only asking you to show me once. Do me this favour, please."

The old monk kept on asking. It was very hard to refuse him. So the Green Dragon said, "Very well, if you insist. I will show you once, but remember this: you must send your pupils far away, or something terrible might happen."

The old monk nodded. "Don't worry, don't worry. Rely on me, rely on me."

Early next morning, he told the two novices, "You are going to buy vegetables in town today. Then go to the Temple of the Three Pagodas and tell your Second Master to come here the day after tomorrow."

One of the novices said, "Master, don't you know it is not market day today? What can we buy?"

"A stupid pupil you are! All kinds of vegetables are sold everyday. Keep quiet! You must obey my order and go where I want you to go. At the Three Pagodas you can have a good time with your fellow novices. You don't have to hurry back. It makes no difference even if you come back after the sun goes down."

The elder novice said, "Well, master, as a rule he buys the vegetables. Are we both to go? Who is going to sweep, and cook, and burn the incense or light the candles?"

"You don't have to bother about such trifles today. I can arrange everything myself. Just go, go, go, both of you go down to buy."

"All right, all right," the two little monks replied in chorus. The old monk saw them off, repeating, "Today both of you may play as long as you like. It is not necessary to return quickly." He watched them start on their way.

Just then the Green Dragon arrived. The old monk was shaking with anticipation. He seized Aiqi by the hand. "It's hard for you. I'm sorry. But as you have seen, I've sent the novices away. There isn't anything to worry about now."

"I hope not," said the Green Dragon. They went into the sitting room. "I thought it over last night. First we must close the gate. Next you must put on the holy robe I gave you. We must be careful."

The old monk agreed. The two friends then went into the courtyard. The gate was locked and the old monk was wearing the holy robe. The monk said

127

excitedly, "Now, my brother Aiqi, show me your green body. Please."

The Green Dragon said nothing but this: "All right. I will show you my ugly body." He said this slowly, but the change happened quick as a lightning flash. In less than half a second, Aiqi's shadow was gone. Instead there was a green creature, about thirty-three centimetres long, with green and golden spots all over its body. It looked much like a snake, but there was a pair of horns on its head. The Green Dragon crept towards the old monk.

At first the monk could see nothing. He called out in a loud voice, "My Dragon God, where are you?" At last he looked down at his feet, and saw the snake. He was very distressed. "Well, well. The mighty dragon turned out to be a spindly little snake. There's nothing so marvellous about a pair of horns. Who'd have thought it? A tiny creature like that able to fly high up in the air, call the rain and wind, blow away the clouds."

As he was speaking, the Green Dragon turned back into a man. "Well, master, are you content?"

The old monk shook his head. "My brother, in my opinion you are a real, no, you are what they call an out-and-out dragon. You ought to be a tremendous creature. I never thought you'd be so puny I could hardly see you."

The Green Dragon laughed. "My respected master, I am not always as little as that. I could make myself as large as I liked, but this time I was afraid you might be scared."

"Ah, no wonder, then. You did it on purpose. Change again. Be quick. Make yourself enormous. I'm afraid of nothing. Dear Aiqi, my mighty Dragon God! Let my eyes enjoy your greatness."

The Green Dragon was flattered. There were no outsiders there, and the monk was wearing his magic garment. He thought there wouldn't be any harm. He said, "Your novices are away. It's a good chance. I'll let you see all you want." The Green Dragon prepared to make himself as large as he could.

Now the two novice monks who had been sent out to buy vegetables didn't walk far. The smaller one turned to the bigger one, and said, "I wonder what our master is planning to do today. Why has he ordered us out of the way? He wanted us to get back after dark. What's going on?"

"There must be some secret, my brother. Just think. As we were about to leave, he reminded us to come back late. Usually we are not allowed to delay a moment. Probably he is doing shameful things in the temple."

It was very strange. As a rule the monk played chess most days with Aiqi. And what do we really know about him? thought the novices. The bigger one would not walk any further. He wanted to know what was going on. He said to the smaller one, "Buying vegetables and visiting Three Pagodas aren't that important. Let's get back and see what is happening in our temple first."

"That's a good idea," the smaller one agreed, and they both turned back to the temple. When they

129

arrived they found the gate tight shut! It was impossible to push it open. But peering through a hole, they saw red and blue rays pulsing from the inner gate. That was all they could see. The smaller one cried, "Brother, we are just in time to see something special today. Our master is doing something extraordinary. Hurry up! Let's get in and have a good look." They ran to fetch a ladder from an outhouse, and quickly climbed in through a window. Looking down into the courtyard the two novices saw an astonishing sight. There was a Green Dragon below. The old monk was shouting and crying. The two little monks watched in silent joy.

The old monk was calling in a thrilled voice, "Bigger! Larger! Longer! Still more!" And the Green Dragon was growing larger and longer. It was already over twenty metres long. Its whole body was glistening with colour. Its horns, claws and tail were shining bright. Just this one dragon took up half the yard. And still the monk wished to see it bigger. Again he shouted, "My Green Dragon, bigger, bigger! The bigger the better."

Now the dragon's head was as big as a grain hopper. Its mouth was as big as a basin. Its teeth were sharp as a knife. Its two eyes bulged like a pair of big bells made of brass. Black stains spotted its body. Now the big yard was too small for the dragon. The old monk had to squat in a corner. He shielded his body with his magic robe, and called in a trembling voice, "All right. That's enough. Stop, please, stop!"

The Green Dragon thought to change himself back

into a man, but he could not. He was at a loss. In his worry and anger he reared his head full seven metres to face the window where the little monks were watching. He let out a terrible scream. The two little ones were struck dead with fright.

A fierce thunderbolt struck down from the blue sky. Thick clouds gathered. Thunder and lightning raged above. The heavens opened, in heavy, ceaseless rain.

The Green Dragon bitterly regretted his carelessness. He could never become a man again. He thrashed his tail, and the main building of the temple was smashed to rubble. With a noise like thousands of horses in a pell-mell race, water roared down the valley to wash away the temple. The Green Dragon was swept sorrowing into Dali Lake. Never again could he walk in human form.

As for the old monk, he too was washed down by the flood, and fetched up at the lake side with his head against a rock. Had he not been wearing the magic robe which the Green Dragon had given him he would surely have died. He wished it had all been a bad dream. He sighed a long sigh for his friend the Green Dragon. But no matter how he wept, the Green Dragon did not rise from the lake.

The old monk felt embarrassed to return to the old place. People would laugh at him. All he could do was wander aimlessly about. Later, people could find no trace or track of him. Where he had gone, nobody knew.

The pond is still there today. Beside it there is a

large square area. This is the site of the old monk's temple. You may clamber on the battered remains of its wall, or pocket a shard of broken tile. Whoever comes to this place will remember this sorrowful story.

"Never Heard of this Before"

Long, long ago, there was a king of the Thai people who had a daughter, the Princess Nanxiang. She was as sleek and beautiful as a mandarin duck. Her eyes were like two pearls shining in pure water. Her voice shamed the nightingale with its beauty. Her name was well-known far and wide.

Now the king loved his daughter more than anything, and dreaded the day she would get married and leave him. He thought that one fine day she would fly far away. So the king tried every way he could to stop her from going out into the world, and kept her shut up inside the palace all the time.

The poor princess could not bear to be shut in. She longed to be able to fly up in the clear blue sky, to find a brave and loving companion and live happy and free.

From time to time princes would come from the four corners of the world to win her love. But the king didn't want her to get married or to live in other

lands, so he plotted to keep her by him. No matter who came, he always said, "I'll only let you marry my daughter if you can tell me something I've never heard before."

One prince said, "Your Majesty, in our country we have a cabbage whose leaves spread over three villages. Its stalks can be used to build a house large enough for the entire population of three kingdoms. You can't have heard of it before." But the king just laughed and said, "Oh yes, I've heard of that before," and sent the young prince packing.

Another prince said, "Most respected king, in our country we have a huge spoon. You can drive in ninety elephants from the right and ninety buffaloes from the left and it still isn't full. Have you ever heard of that before?" The king gave a little smile as if that was a very ordinary thing, "I heard of that a long time ago." He sent the young prince about his business.

Yet another prince came, and said, "Most honourable king, in our country we have a huge rice bowl which stands on the earth and holds up the sky. If there is a storm, all the people can huddle beneath it. You too are welcome to shelter there. I'm sure your Majesty never heard of this before?" The king gave a careless shrug, "Oh, thanks for your kindness, but I've heard of this many many times." He showed the young prince the door.

The king turned away all the princes who came to propose marriage. With the same answer, "I've heard this before," all the young princes were refused. He still insisted on locking his daughter inside the palace, though she loved the open air. Princess Nanxiang was very sad. She hated her father, but she could do nothing to stop those handsome princes riding away. The whole country pitied her, the old people as well as the young men, but nobody could help her.

In a certain village there lived a handsome young man called Aiwang. His home was a poor one, and he lived by weaving bamboo baskets and cutting wood. One day he went to sell firewood in town. People there told him how the king mistreated his daughter, keeping her like a rare bird in a cage. It would surely be a wonderful thing to rescue such a beautiful and noble princess and marry her.

Aiwang thought and thought about this and finally came to a decision. Early the next day he rushed to the hillside and returned with a lot of bamboo. In seven days he made seven large baskets. Then he asked seven friends to carry them into the king's palace. They marched through the gate and set the seven baskets down in the courtyard.

The king was quite puzzled by this display. He scolded Aiwang, "You poor rascal! Fancy bringing so many people with empty baskets into my courtyard. What's the meaning of it?"

Standing in front of the powerful king, Aiwang said quietly, "Don't abuse the poor, and be ungrateful as well as a cheat, Your Majesty. My father has told me all the facts."

"Facts?" said the king.

"I'm coming to them," said Aiwang. He paused, and then continued, "Everybody knows you are rich and powerful and I am only a poor peasant. But everybody knows why, too."

"Why?" said the king.

"I won't waste your time. In a word, your grand-father's grandfather borrowed seven basketfuls of silver and gold from my grandfather's grandfather. That's the only reason why you are rich and I am poor. And that's all I've got to say. I've come for my gold and silver. It's high time you returned it. Here are my seven baskets . . ."

The king was knocked sideways by the news. "I'm much older than you are, and have seen and heard many things, but I can tell you I've never heard of this before."

Cunning Aiwang turned to his friends. "Did you hear that? What did the king say?"

"He said, 'I've never heard of this before.'"

The king nodded, "Yes, that's right. That's what I said."

And then the king realized what he had done. He felt very awkward, and didn't know what to say or do next. He knew he had made a big blunder. He wanted to take back his words, but it was too late.

Princess Nanxiang realized what he had done, too. She looked at Aiwang, and felt her heart leap within her.

The oldest of Aiwang's friends then said, "Allow me to ask our wise and mighty king one question. Had you ever heard the facts that Aiwang related just now? If so, hurry up and empty your treasure into those seven baskets. If not, just let your princess marry Aiwang, as you promised."

"Yes, hurry up, the silver or the princess," shouted the others. The king was struck dumb, and could only stare wildly around him. But nothing in his grand palace could tell him what to say, so he just repeated, "Truly, I've never heard of this before."

The beautiful Nanxiang walked towards Aiwang, and Aiwang walked towards her. Everyone cheered. Alone in a throng of friends, they walked out of the palace hand in hand.

Notes on the stories

The stories have been selected from three Chinese volumes:
Folktales of China (Part One) (People's Literature Publishing
House, Peking, 1958)
Fifty Tales of Yunnan (ed. Wang Shouchun, Yunnan People's
Publishing house, Kunming, 1979)
A Collection of Folktales of Yunnan National Minorities (Literature
of Yunnan Masses, Kunming, 1979)
They were collected either in the first flush of Communist
enthusiasm for folk literature in the 1950s, or since the downfall of the "Gang of Four" in 1978. Where details of narrator or
collector were provided, these are noted below. They represent
only a fragment of a great mass of material, published and
unpublished. Richard Dorson noted in his foreword to the best
introduction to the Chinese tale, Wolfram Eberhard's *The
Folktales of China* (Routledge and Kegan Paul/University of
Chicago Press, 1965), that, "a fieldwork team in the Yunnan
area within six months in 1958 accumulated more than a
hundred thousand items of folk literature and folk culture."

The Wonderful Brocade (Zhuang)
Unlike most of the others in this book, this story has appeared
in several publications in English translation, notably as "The

Piece of Chuang Brocade" in *Folk Tales from China*, Third Series (Foreign Language Press, Peking, 1958) and as "The Wonderful Chuang Brocade" in M. A. Jagendorf and Virginia Weng *The Magic Boat and other Chinese Folk Stories* (The Vanguard Press, New York, 1980), which includes helpful notes on China's ethnic minorities. In both these translations, and in He Liyi's original text, the creatures I have called "spirit maidens" are referred to as "fairies", which I felt was culturally clumsy. The tree is a strawberry-tree *(Arbutus unedo)*.

The Spring of Butterflies (Bai)
Arranged by Yin Ching
There are many stories of Lu Ban, who is a patron of carpenters and craftsmen.

The Tibetan Envoy (Tibetan)
Arranged by Shao Chongsu
Translated as "The Tibetan Envoy's Mission" in *The Magic Boat*. Jagendorf and Weng note that, "Emperor T'ai-tsung married his kinswoman Princess Wen-ch'eng to the first king of Tibet after he repelled an invasion by Tibet in 641." He Liyi's text has another paragraph at the end describing the changes wrought in Tibet by the new grains and by the experts in agriculture and architecture whom the princess takes with her as a dowry.

The Dougarda Brothers (Thai)
It is my addition that Bosankang sees a glint of gold when Big Dougarda removes the coin.

A Woman's Love (Uighur)
Told by Smae Yolerda, collected and arranged by Liu Saofu
Translated as "A Clever Woman" in *Folk Tales from China*, Third Series.
The Uighur are Moslem, with a settled agricultural life unlike that of the nomadic Kazak. I have slightly condensed this tale

142

between kidnap and rescue. In the original the episode of the "Bird of Happiness" is very obscure. The incident is paralleled in a short tale recorded from an Iraqi storyteller in Israel, "A Servant When He Reigns", *Folktales of Israel* ed. Dov Noy (Routledge and Kegan Paul/ University of Chicago Press, 1963).

The Princess's Veil (Uighur)
Told by Wunamarji, collected by Zen Baitao
This story needed more editorial interference than the others; the father seems to change his mind half way through, as perhaps fathers do, as to whether he wishes his daughter to marry or not. So I have made the young man "ragged" to provide a motive for this change of heart. My "good-for-nothing" substitutes for He Liyi's mysterious "poor ghost".

The King and a Poor Man (Kazak)
The method of staying alive underground is my own invention; the original takes no account of breathing.

The Story of Washing Horse Pond (Bai)
Arranged by Yang Cheng
Another story translated by He Liyi, the Mongol "Hunter Hailibu", also has a hero turned to stone in saving others.

A Crane and Two Brothers (Tulong)
Told by Li Ximing, arranged by Bai Chusuo
The original title is "Mount Sun". He Liyi notes that this tale is still often told among the Tulong.

A Stone Sheep (Yi)
Arranged by Liu Guirong
The Yi are also known as the Lolo. Dragons in China are associated with water and rain, not fire. The tears which break the stone seal are my invention, as is the statement that the

dragon is too lazy to make rain; the original merely says his behaviour is "notorious" and leaves it at that.

A Golden Fish (Uighur)
This story seems allied to the widespread "Grateful Dead" tales in which the mysterious helper is the ghost of a man for whose funeral the hero has paid.

The Two Brothers (Naxi)
Arranged by Yang Zai
A similar version of this tale, identified as "a story of the Tong people", is given as "How the Brothers Divided Their Property" in *Folk Tales from China*, First Series (Foreign Languages Press, Peking, 1957). The melon incident is duplicated in another story translated by He Liyi, but not included here, "A Big Pumpkin", also narrated by Li Ximing the teller of "A Crane and Two Brothers". The winter melon is a variety of muskmelon.

Green Dragon Pond (Bai)
Arranged by Yang Guangyong
There is a similar story, also Bai, in which the importunate friend dies from fright when he sees the dragon's true form, in *Folk Tales from China,* Fourth Series (Foreign Languages Press, Peking, 1958), "The Dragon King of Langchong".

"Never Heard of This Before" (Thai)
Arranged by San Bao
The Thai are the mother people of the Thais of Thailand. This tale shows a very pleasing comic spirit in their storytelling.